french fancies

french fancies

and other adorable
bite-size bakes

RYLAND PETERS & SMALL
LONDON • NEW YORK

Designer Maria Lee-Warren
Editor Rebecca Woods
Production Gary Hayes
Art Director Leslie Harrington
Editorial Director Julia Charles

Indexer Hilary Bird

First published in 2013 by
Ryland Peters & Small
20–21 Jockey's Fields,
London WC1R 4BW
and
Ryland Peters & Small Inc.
519 Broadway, 5th Floor
New York, NY 10012

www.rylandpeters.com
10 9 8 7 6 5 4 3 2 1

Text © Susannah Blake, Claire Burnet, Maxine Clark,
Julian Day, Lydia France, Carol Hilker, Hannah Miles,
Annie Rigg, 2013

Design and photographs © Ryland Peters
& Small 2013

ISBN: 978-1-84975-426-2

A CIP record for this book is available from the British Library.

US Library of Congress cataloguing-in-publication data has been
applied for.

Printed and bound in China

Notes
• All spoon measurements are level unless otherwise specified.
• Eggs used in this book are UK medium/US large, unless
otherwise specified. Free-range eggs are recommended.
Uncooked or partly cooked eggs should not be served
to the very young, the very old, those with compromised
immune systems or to pregnant women.
• Ovens should be preheated to the specified temperatures. All
ovens work slightly differently. We recommend using an oven
thermometer and suggest you consult the maker's handbook
for any special instructions, particularly if you are cooking in
a fan-assisted/convection oven, as you will need to adjust
temperatures according to manufacturer's instructions.

contents

a little bit of what you fancy...

An adorable sweet treat, home-baked and presented or served with thought, can say a great many things: a tray of colourful macarons will show mum how much she is appreciated on Mother's day; a bag of fun strawberry malt marshmallows can say 'cheer up' to a friend; while sugar love-heart cookies can say those three important little words on Valentine's Day. Whatever the occasion, never let a celebration pass without one of these delightfully delicious dainties!

Baking is one of the most pleasurable ways to pass time, and the smiles that these treats will be greeted with will only add to the satisfaction. The French fancies and other tiny treats in this book are designed to thrill the taste buds in just one or two mouthfuls. Each chapter contains different types of bite-size bakes – from pretty-as-a-picture cakes to light-as-air pastries, whimsical whoopie pies to irresistible marshmallows. While brownie pops will light up little faces at a child's birthday celebration, classic millefeuilles are stylish enough to serve at an elegant afternoon tea party, and sophisticated salted caramel tartlets will impress served with coffee at a smart dinner.

You don't need a huge amount of skill or an enormous variety of kitchen equipment to make the recipes in this book. All the treats can be baked using mini cupcake, muffin and tartlet pans, which are widely available from good cookware stores. Just follow the simple recipe steps, which will guide you clearly through the process. And as with any baking, always try to use the best and freshest ingredients you can afford – fresh free range eggs, good quality chocolate, fresh fruits and nuts.

So why not don your apron, grab your whisk and whip up a batch of delightfully tiny treats today!

cakes & bakes

French fancies are just one of the classic bakes in the daintiest of dimensions to grace this chapter. Mini cupcakes and iced gem cakes both look pretty swirled with mixed and matched pastel frostings and topped with cheerfully coloured sprinkles. Cute cake pops can be dressed to suit your mood, while pretty-as-a-picture cakes include beautiful butterfly cakes dusted with sugar, mini blueberry bundts served with a sweet berry drizzling sauce, and perfectly proportioned strawberry and cream layer cakes topped with the sweetest fondant strawberries. Perfect for afternoon tea parties and elegant dinners, these cakes also make welcome and thoughtful gifts.

french fancies

These little pretty pastel cakes topped with sugared petals are just perfect. Tiny morsels of sweet cake, delicately scented with rose and violet, they will delight any afternoon tea party guest.

115 g/1 stick butter, softened
115 g/½ cup plus 1 tablespoon caster/granulated sugar
2 eggs
115 g/¾ cup plus 1 tablespoon self-raising flour
1 tablespoon plain yogurt
1 teaspoon vanilla extract

for the buttercream
300 g/2 cups icing/confectioners' sugar
30 g/2 tablespoons butter, softened
1–2 tablespoons milk
4 tablespoons violet liqueur

to decorate
500 g/3¾ cups powdered fondant icing sugar
2 tablespoons rose syrup
pink and blue food colouring
candied rose and violet petals

a cake pan (20 cm/8 inches square), greased and lined with baking parchment
a piping bag fitted with a small round nozzle/tip
20 petits fours cases

makes 20

Preheat the oven to 180°C (350°F) Gas 4.

To make the sponge cake, whisk together the butter and sugar until light and creamy. Add the eggs and whisk again. Sift in the flour and fold in, along with the yogurt and vanilla extract. Spoon the mixture into the prepared cake pan and bake in the preheated oven for 20–25 minutes, until the cake is golden brown and springs back to the touch. Leave to cool.

To make the buttercream, whisk together the icing/confectioners' sugar, butter, milk and 1 tablespoon of the violet liqueur until light and creamy.

Trim away the sides of the cake, then cut the cake in half horizontally. Place one cake half on a tray that will fit in the refrigerator. Drizzle the remaining violet liqueur over the sponge cake and spread over a thin layer of buttercream. Top with the other half and cover the top and sides of the cake with a thin layer of buttercream.

Using a sharp knife, score the top of the cake into 20 squares (do not cut through to the cake). Spoon the remaining buttercream into the piping bag and pipe a small blob of buttercream in the middle of each square. Chill in the refrigerator for 2 hours, until the buttercream is firm, then cut the cake into the marked squares.

Put the fondant icing sugar in a saucepan with 3–4 tablespoons water, the rose syrup and a few drops of pink food colouring. (Add the water gradually as you may not need it all.) Put the cakes on a wire rack with foil underneath to catch the drips. Spoon the warm icing over half of the cakes, ensuring each cake is covered completely. When you have iced half the cakes, add a few drops of blue food colouring to the remaining icing to make a lilac colour and cover the remaining cakes.

Decorate each cake with a rose or violet petal and leave to set before putting in paper cases, to serve.

mini cupcakes

115 g/1 stick butter, softened
115 g/½ cup plus 1 tablespoon
   caster/granulated sugar
grated zest of 1 lemon
2 eggs
115 g/¾ cup plus 1 tablespoon
   self-raising flour

for the buttercream
175 g/1½ sticks unsalted butter,
   softened
450 g/3⅓ cups icing/
   confectioners' sugar, sifted
3 tablespoons freshly squeezed
   lemon juice
food colouring(s) in your choice
   of colour

to decorate
sugar sprinkles
silver dragées

*a 24-hole mini muffin pan, lined with
   paper cases*
*1–2 piping bags fitted with large star
   nozzles/tips*

makes 24

Mix and match the colours of the frosting swirls and sugar sprinkles on these baby cupcakes for a pretty pastel masterpiece that will look almost too good to eat. Packaged in decorative boxes, they make a lovely gift, too.

Preheat the oven to 180°C (350°F) Gas 4.

In a large mixing bowl, beat together the butter and sugar until pale and creamy. Beat in the lemon zest and then the eggs, one at a time. Sift the flour over the mixture, then fold everything together thoroughly.

Spoon the cake mixture into the paper cases and bake in the preheated oven for about 15 minutes, until risen and golden and the sponge bounces back when gently pressed with a fingertip. Transfer the cakes to a wire rack and set aside to cool completely.

To make the buttercream, beat together the butter, icing/confectioners' sugar and lemon juice with an electric hand whisk until smooth and creamy. Tint the buttercream with a few drops of the food colouring of your choice (or divide between two bowls and tint two different colours) and briefly beat again to achieve an even colour.

Spoon the frosting into the piping bag and pipe a swirl on top of each of the cupcakes. (Repeat with the second batch of frosting, if using two colours.) Scatter each cupcake with sugar sprinkles and finish with a silver dragée.

strawberry & cream layer cakes

- 115 g/½ cup plus 1 tablespoon caster/granulated sugar
- 115 g/1 stick butter, softened
- 2 eggs
- 85 g/⅔ cup self-raising flour
- 30 g/⅓ cup ground almonds
- 1 teaspoon vanilla extract
- 300 ml/1¼ cups double/heavy cream, whipped
- 200 g/1½ cups strawberries, thinly sliced
- 3 generous tablespoons strawberry jam/jelly

to decorate
- 30 g/1 oz. ready-to-roll fondant icing
- red and green food colouring pastes
- 200 g/1⅔ cups powdered fondant icing sugar
- 1 tablespoon rosewater

10 mini cake pans (6 cm/2½ inches diameter), greased

makes 10

What could be nicer than having a whole layer cake all to yourself? Decorated with tiny handmade fondant strawberries, these little treats are pretty-as-a-picture and perfect for any summer tea party.

Preheat the oven to 180°C (350°F) Gas 4.

In a mixing bowl, whisk together the sugar and butter until light and creamy. Whisk in the eggs then sift in the flour. Fold in along with the almonds and vanilla extract. Spoon the mixture into the prepared cake pans and bake in the preheated oven for 15–20 minutes, until the cakes spring back to the touch. Leave to cool in the pans, then slide a knife around the edge of each one to release the cakes.

To make the fondant strawberries, colour three quarters of the ready-to-roll icing red with a small amount of red food colouring paste. Colour the remainder with the green food colouring paste. Make at least 40 tiny strawberry shapes with the red icing and use a clean pin to prick holes in them to look like the seeds. Top each with a tiny blob of green icing to represent the stalks. Set aside to dry.

To prepare the icing, mix together the fondant icing sugar, rosewater and about 1 tablespoon cold water until you have a smooth, thick icing. Cut each cake into 3 layers and cover the top layer of each cake with icing. Allow the icing to set for about 5 minutes, then gently press 4 fondant strawberries on to the top of each one to decorate.

Once the icing has set completely, assemble the cakes. Spoon a little whipped cream and preserve between each layer, topping with strawberry slices. Finish each one with an iced and decorated top.

Serve immediately or store in the refrigerator until needed.

iced gem cakes

350 g/2⅔ cups plain/all-purpose
    flour
3 teaspoons baking powder
I teaspoon bicarbonate of
    soda/baking soda
a pinch of salt
225 g/2 sticks butter, softened
350 g/1¾ cups caster/granulated
    sugar
4 large eggs
I teaspoon vanilla extract
250 ml/1 cup buttermilk, at
    room temperature
4 tablespoons strawberry jam

for the meringue buttercream
275 g/1⅓ cups caster/superfine
    sugar
4 large egg whites
a pinch of salt
350 g/3 sticks butter, softened
    and diced
I teaspoon vanilla extract or the
    seeds from ½ vanilla pod/bean

to decorate
assorted food colouring pastes
sugar sprinkles
assorted, coloured gummy
    sweets/candies

a baking pan (20 x 30 x 4 cm/
    8 x 12 x 1¾ inches), greased
    and lined with greased baking
    parchment
a 6–7-cm/2½–3-inch round cookie
    cutter
a piping bag fitted with a star
    nozzle/tip
a sugar thermometer

makes 12

Sometimes smaller is better, and these little gems of cake are no exception. They are perfect for a kids' party, as they are just enough for little hands and they can be packaged into pretty boxes to take away as favours. They do need to be prepared a day in advance, so plan accordingly. However, that does mean you will have less to worry about on the day of the party!

Preheat the oven to 180°C (350°F) Gas 4.

Sift together the flour, baking powder, bicarbonate of soda/baking soda and salt.

Cream the butter and sugar in the bowl of a stand mixer until really pale and light – at least 3–4 minutes.

Lightly beat the eggs and vanilla together. Gradually add to the creamed butter in 4 or 5 additions, mixing well between each addition and scraping down the bowl from time to time with a spatula. Add the sifted dry ingredients to the bowl alternately with the buttermilk. Mix until smooth.

Pour the cake batter into the prepared baking pan and spread level. Bake on the middle shelf of the preheated oven for about 30 minutes or until a skewer inserted into the middle of the cake comes out clean. Leave to cool in the pan for 3–4 minutes, then turn out onto a wire rack to cool completely. When cold, wrap the cake in clingfilm/ plastic wrap and set aside until the following day.

The next day, when you are ready to assemble the cake, gently heat the strawberry jam to make it a little runnier, then pass it through a sieve/strainer to get rid of any lumps.

Unwrap the cake and use the cookie cutter to stamp out 12 circles. Brush the sides of each cake with a little of the jam.

To make the meringue buttercream, put the sugar, egg whites and salt in a medium heatproof bowl set over a pan of simmering water. Whisk slowly with a balloon whisk until the sugar has completely dissolved and the mixture is foamy. Continue to cook and whisk until the mixture reaches 60°C/140°F on a sugar thermometer – about 4 minutes.

Quickly pour the mixture into the bowl of a stand mixer and whisk on medium– high speed for 3 minutes, or until cooled, thick, stiff and glossy. Gradually add the butter, beating constantly, until the frosting is smooth. Fold in the vanilla and use immediately.

Divide the buttercream between 4 bowls and tint each one a different colour using the food colouring pastes. Using a palette knife, spread some meringue buttercream neatly around the side of each cake. Roll the sides in sugar sprinkles until evenly coated.

Spoon one colour of buttercream into the piping bag and pipe a lovely swirl on top of each cake. Repeat with the remaining buttercream and cakes. Press a gummy sweet/candy on the top of each cake just before serving.

mini blueberry bundts

60 g/⅓ cup caster/granulated
   sugar
60 g/½ stick butter, softened
1 egg
60 g/½ cup self-raising flour
1 teaspoon baking powder
60 g/½ cup blueberries,
   quartered
finely grated zest of 2 lemons

to decorate
250 g/2½ cups blueberries
freshly squeezed juice of
   2 lemons
150 g/¾ cup caster/granulated
   sugar

24 mini bundt ring pans (7 cm/
   2¾ inches diameter), greased

makes 24

Traditional German Bundt cakes are popular the world over. Bundt pans are ring pans usually decorated with patterned edges and it is important to grease the pans well so that the cakes release. Topped with a blueberry drizzle and fresh berries, these tiny bundts are almost too cute to eat!

Preheat the oven to 180°C (350°F) Gas 4.

Put the sugar and butter in a mixing bowl and beat together until light and creamy, then whisk in the egg. Sift in the flour and baking powder and gently fold in, along with the quartered blueberries and lemon zest.

Spoon the mixture into the prepared bundt pans and bake in the preheated oven for 12–15 minutes, until the cakes spring back to your touch. Remove the cakes from the pans and leave to cool on a wire rack.

To make the blueberry drizzle, cut 50 g/½ cup of the blueberries in half and put them in a pan with the lemon juice. Heat gently until the blueberries are very soft and have released their juices. Strain through a sieve/strainer, pressing down on the fruit to release all the juices. Return the strained juice to the pan, add the sugar and stir over the heat until the sugar is dissolved.

Drizzle the blueberry syrup over the cakes and fill the central holes of the cakes with the remaining fresh blueberries to serve.

butterfly cakes

100 g/6½ tablespoons salted
   butter, softened
100 g/½ cup caster/granulated
   sugar
grated zest of 1 orange
2 eggs
100 g/¾ cup self-raising flour

for the orange filling
100 g/6½ tablespoons salted
   butter, softened
200 g/1⅓ cups icing/
   confectioners' sugar
grated zest of 1 orange, plus
   the freshly squeezed juice
   of ½ orange

*a 12-hole muffin pan, lined with
paper cupcake cases
a piping bag (optional)*

makes 12

Perfect for coffee mornings, bake sales and an absolute must for children's parties, these pretty cakes look great and are quick and easy to make. Ring the changes by making a selection of flavours; shown below is the recipe for orange, with vanilla and chocolate variations, but you could try coffee or lemon, too.

Preheat the oven to 190°C (375°F) Gas 5.

Using an electric hand whisk, cream together the butter, sugar and orange zest in a large mixing bowl until pale and fluffy. Add the eggs one at a time, beating well between each addition. With the whisk on slow speed, gradually add the flour to achieve a smooth consistency.

Spoon the mixture into the paper cases and bake in the preheated oven for 12–15 minutes or until golden brown and the tops spring back to the touch. Remove from the oven and transfer to a wire rack to cool.

To make the orange filling, beat the butter, icing/confectioners' sugar, orange juice and zest together with an electric hand whisk. Start on slow speed and increase to high speed when all the sugar is incorporated, beating for about 2–3 minutes in total.

When the cakes have cooled, slice the tops off them, then cut each top in half to form wings. Pipe or spoon the buttercream onto the top of the cakes and place the wings on top. Dust icing/confectioners' sugar over them.

Vanilla variation: Add ¼ teaspoon vanilla extract in place of the orange zest. For the vanilla filling, mix 1 teaspoon vanilla extract and 2 tablespoons water together and add to the butter and sugar in place of the orange juice and zest.

Chocolate variation: Stir 1 tablespoon cocoa powder and 1 tablespoon water together to form a paste and add to the butter and sugar in place of the orange zest. For the chocolate filling, mix 2 tablespoons cocoa powder and 1 tablespoon water together to form a paste and add to butter and sugar in place of orange juice and zest.

white chocolate cake pops

These cuter-than-cute cake pops have a fudgy centre and crisp white chocolate coating. They are delicious and very easy to make, especially if you buy a ready-made cake.

2 tablespoons double/heavy cream

25 g/2 tablespoons butter, softened

100 g/3 ½ oz. white chocolate, broken into chunks

175 g/6 oz. plain sponge/pound cake, such as **Madeira cake**, finely crumbled

to decorate

200 g/7 oz. white chocolate, broken into chunks

sugar sprinkles

20 lollipop/popsicle sticks

makes 20

Put the cream, butter and the 100 g/ 3½ oz. white chocolate in a heatproof bowl set over a pan of barely simmering water. Leave to stand until melted, then remove from the heat and stir in the cake crumbs. Chill in the refrigerator for about 1 hour, until firm.

Take generous teaspoonfuls of the mixture and roll into balls roughly the size of a small walnut. Gently insert a lollipop/popsicle stick into each one then leave to chill and set overnight.

To decorate, break the 200 g/7 oz. white chocolate into a heatproof bowl and melt over a pan of barely simmering water. Remove from the heat and leave the chocolate to cool and thicken. Dip the cake pops in the chocolate, turning to coat, then decorate with the sprinkles. Leave to set before serving.

summer berry cupcakes

Topped with a cascade of summer berries and a swirl of strawberry-scented, delicate pink buttercream, these cupcakes are the height of summer sophistication. You could also top the cakes with just one type of fruit if you prefer.

175 g/1½ sticks butter, softened

200 g/1 cup caster/granulated sugar

2 whole eggs and 1 egg yolk, beaten

1 teaspoon vanilla extract

225 g/1¾ cups plain/all-purpose flour

1 teaspoon baking powder

½ teaspoon bicarbonate of soda/baking soda

125 ml/½ cup buttermilk

for the strawberry meringue buttercream

200 g/1 cup caster/granulated sugar

3 egg whites

250 g/2 sticks unsalted butter, softened and cubed

1 teaspoon vanilla extract

3–4 tablespoons sieved/strained strawberry jam/jelly

to decorate

assorted summer berries, such as strawberries, raspberries, blueberries and redcurrants

icing/confectioners' sugar, for dusting

1–2 muffin pans, lined with paper cupcake cases

a sugar thermometer

makes 12–16

Preheat the oven to 180°C (350°F) Gas 4.

In a large mixing bowl, cream together the butter and sugar until light and creamy. Gradually add the beaten eggs, mixing well between each addition and scraping down the side of the mixing bowl from time to time. Add the vanilla.

Sift together the flour, baking powder and bicarbonate of soda/baking soda and add to the mixture in alternate batches with the buttermilk. Mix until smooth.

Divide the cake batter between the cupcake cases, filling them two-thirds full, and bake on the middle shelf of the preheated oven for 20 minutes, or until well risen and a skewer inserted into the middle of the cupcakes comes out clean. Leave to cool in the pans for 5 minutes before transferring to a wire rack to cool completely.

To make the meringue buttercream, put the sugar and egg whites in a heatproof bowl set over a pan of simmering water. Whisk until it reaches at least 60°C (140°F) on the sugar thermometer. Pour into the bowl of a stand mixer fitted with the whisk attachment (or use an electric hand whisk and mixing bowl). Beat until the mixture has doubled in volume, cooled and will stand in stiff, glossy peaks – this will take about 3 minutes.

Gradually add the butter to the cooled meringue mix, beating constantly, until the frosting is smooth, then fold in the vanilla and the strawberry jam/jelly.

Spread the meringue buttercream over the cold cupcakes and arrange the berries on top of each one in a lovely cascade. Dust with icing/confectioners' sugar, to finish.

mini carrot muffins

Who doesn't love a slice of moist carrot cake with a fluffy, cream cheese frosting? These mini mouthfuls are packed with pistachios, walnuts and coconut and make a delightfully wholesome anytime treat.

60 g/¼ cup (packed) soft dark brown sugar
60 g/½ stick butter, softened
1 large egg
60 g/½ cup self-raising flour
1 teaspoon ground cinnamon
1 teaspoon ground mixed spice/apple pie spice
finely grated zest of ½ orange
1 teaspoon vanilla extract
1 carrot, peeled and cut into chunks
30 g/¼ cup unsalted pistachio kernels
30 g/¼ cup walnut pieces
1 generous tablespoon long shredded coconut

for the cream cheese frosting
50 g/¼ cup cream cheese
25 g/2 tablespoons butter, softened
85 g/½ cup icing/confectioners' sugar
finely grated zest of ½ orange
20 edible carrot cake toppers, to decorate (optional)

a 24-hole mini muffin pan, greased
a piping bag fitted with a large star nozzle/tip

makes 20

Preheat the oven to 180°C (350°F) Gas 4.

In a large mixing bowl, whisk together the brown sugar and butter until light and creamy. Beat in the egg and then sift in the flour, cinnamon and mixed spice/apple pie spice. Fold in along with the orange zest and vanilla extract.

Put the carrot chunks, pistachios, walnuts and coconut in the bowl of a food processor and chop very finely. (If you do not have a food processor, grate the carrot and chop the nuts finely using a sharp knife.) Fold the carrot mixture into the cake mixture until everything is incorporated.

Spoon the mixture into the prepared muffin pan and bake in the preheated oven for 12–15 minutes, until the muffins spring back to the touch. Turn out onto a wire rack to cool.

To make the cream cheese frosting, whisk together the cream cheese, butter, icing/confectioners' sugar and orange zest. Spoon into the piping bag and pipe a swirl of frosting on top of each muffin. To decorate, top each muffin with a carrot cake topper (if using).

lilac & lavender petit fours

You will need to bake the cake layers for these little cakes one day before you plan to decorate them. They will be much easier to cut into neat squares the day after baking. Dried lavender is now available from some supermarkets and sugarcraft suppliers, but if you use your own, make sure it is unsprayed and uncoloured. Serve these little cakes at a sophisticated afternoon tea — Mother's Day would be a perfect occasion.

150 g/1 cup plus 3 tablespoons
plain/all-purpose flour
25 g/¼ cup ground almonds
2 teaspoons baking powder
½ teaspoon bicarbonate of
soda/baking soda
a pinch of salt
175 g/¾ cup caster/granulated
sugar
2 teaspoons dried lavender
flowers
175 g/1½ sticks butter, softened
3 large eggs, lightly beaten
grated zest of ½ lemon
3 tablespoons sour cream,
at room temperature
4–5 tablespoons apricot jam/jelly
4 tablespoons good lemon curd

to decorate
500 g/1 lb. ready-to-roll
fondant icing
lilac food colouring paste
icing/confectioners' sugar,
to dust
tubes of green and purple
writing icing

2 square cake pans (20 cm/8 inches
square), greased and baselined
with baking parchment
2 disposable piping bags
ribbons

makes 9

Start making the cake the day before you want to serve it. Preheat the oven to 180°C (350°F) Gas 4.

Sift together the flour, ground almonds, baking powder, bicarbonate of soda/baking soda and salt.

Whizz the sugar and lavender in a food processor for 10 seconds. This will bring out the lovely lavender fragrance.

Cream the butter and lavender sugar in the bowl of a stand mixer until really pale and light — at least 3–4 minutes. Gradually add the beaten eggs to the creamed butter in 4 or 5 additions, mixing well between each addition and scraping down the bowl from time to time with a rubber spatula. Add the lemon zest, sifted dry ingredients and sour cream and mix until smooth. Divide the mixture evenly between the prepared cake pans and spread level. Bake the cakes on the middle shelf of the preheated oven for about 20 minutes or until a skewer inserted into the middle comes out clean. Leave to cool in the pans for 3–4 minutes, then turn out onto a wire rack and leave to cool completely. Wrap the cold cakes in clingfilm/plastic wrap and set aside until the following day.

The next day, when you are ready to assemble the cake, gently heat the apricot jam/jelly to make it a little runnier, then strain it to get rid of any lumps.

Place one of the cake layers on a work surface and spread the lemon curd over it, then cover with the other cake. Gently press the cakes together. Trim the edges if they need neatening, then cut into 9 even cubes. Brush the top and sides of each cube with the jam.

Tint the ready-to-roll fondant icing a delicate shade of lilac using the food colouring paste. Divide it into 9 even pieces and, on a surface lightly dusted with icing/confectioners' sugar, roll each piece out into a square roughly 2 mm/1/16 inch thick. Cover each cake cube with a square of the icing, using your hands to smooth the top and sides. Trim off any excess icing and let the cakes dry on a board.

Using the green writing icing, pipe 3 stalks and 2 leaves for the lavender on top of each cake. Use the purple icing to pipe the lavender flowers on each stalk.

Let the icing dry completely before tying a pretty ribbon around the bottom edge of each cake.

floral baby cake bites

These pretty bite–size cakes make wonderful petits fours and look lovely arranged in paper cases on an elegant cake stand. Use ready–made sugar flower decorations, which look professional and make your life a lot simpler! Most cake decorating shops and online stockists have a beautiful selection to choose from.

115 g/1 stick butter, softened

115 g/½ cup plus 1 tablespoon caster/granulated sugar

2 eggs

½ teaspoon vanilla extract

115 g/¾ cup plus 1 tablespoon self-raising flour

2 tablespoons raspberry jam/jelly

to decorate

600 g/4½ cups icing/confectioners' sugar

1 tablespoon golden syrup/light corn syrup

½ teaspoon vanilla extract

blue, yellow and pink food colouring

ready-made sugar flowers

2 cake pans (20 cm/8 inches square), greased and lined with baking parchment

petits fours cases

makes 49

Preheat the oven to 180°C (350°F) Gas 4.

In a large mixing bowl, beat together the butter and sugar until pale and creamy. Beat in the eggs one at a time, then stir in the vanilla extract. Sift the flour over the mixture, then fold everything together.

Divide the mixture between the prepared cake pans and bake in the preheated oven for about 13 minutes, until risen and the top springs back when gently pressed with a fingertip. Turn the cakes out onto a wire rack and leave to cool.

Once cooled, spread a thin layer of jam over one cake and place the second cake on top, patting down. Using a sharp knife, gently slice the cake into 7 strips, then slice into 7 strips in the opposite direction. Arrange the cubes on the wire rack, spacing well apart.

Put the icing/confectioners' sugar, golden syrup/light corn syrup, vanilla extract and 4½ tablespoons water in a bowl and stir to combine. Divide the mixture between three heatproof bowls and tint each a different colour. Place one bowl over a pan of barely simmering water, stirring, for 3 minutes. If the icing remains very thick, add a drop of water at a time until you achieve a pouring consistency. Working quickly, spoon the icing over one-third of the cakes and top each with a sugar flower whilst still sticky. (If the icing becomes hard, return to the heat briefly until thinned.) Repeat with the remaining icing and cake cubes, returning each to the wire rack to set. When the icing is dry, place each cake in a petit four case, to serve.

cookies & brownies

From sophisticated biscotti to elegant sugar hearts, zesty lemon cookies to delicately spiced gingerbread, there is no better accompaniment to a relaxing cup of tea or coffee than a cookie. While the mint chocolate kisses make the perfect Valentine's gift, kids will love the popcorn cookies studded with popcorn kernels, nuts and chocolate chunks. For even more indulgence, brownies — those rich gooey squares of chocolate decadence — take so little effort for so much satisfaction. Dress them up with gold dragées and serve them in small squares as an after-dinner delicacy, or add a lollipop stick for a fun children's treat that are as irresistible to behold as they are to taste. And if you can't decide between cookies or brownies, brookies offer the very best of both!

ribboned sugar cookies

These simple buttery cookies look so pretty mixed and matched.
Threaded with ribbon, they make a perfect Valentine's Day gift.

115 g/1 stick butter, softened
50 g/¼ cup caster/granulated
   sugar, plus extra for sprinkling
1 egg yolk
175 g/1⅓ cups plain/all-purpose
   flour
2 tablespoons milk, to glaze

to decorate
200 g/7 oz. ready-to-roll
   fondant icing
2 tablespoons apricot jam/jelly,
   sieved/strained
edible gold lustre

a 7.5-cm/3-inch heart cookie cutter
2 baking sheets, lined with baking
   parchment
a drinking straw
a soft-bristled brush
14 lengths of organza ribbon

makes 14

In a large mixing bowl, cream together the butter and sugar, then beat in the egg yolk. Sift the flour over the mixture and stir well to combine. Tip the mixture out onto a lightly floured surface and knead gently to make a soft dough. Wrap in clingfilm/plastic wrap and chill in the refrigerator for 30 minutes.

Preheat the oven to 180°C (350°F) Gas 4.

Roll out the dough on a lightly floured surface to about 6 mm/¼ inch thick. Stamp out hearts using the cutter and arrange on the prepared baking sheets. If making simple sugar-sprinkled cookies, use a pastry brush to lightly glaze the top of each cookie with milk and then sprinkle them generously with sugar, otherwise, leave them bare. Make a hole at the top of each cookie with the straw, then bake the cookies in the preheated oven for about 10 minutes or until pale golden. Leave to cool on the baking sheets for a few minutes, then transfer to a wire rack to cool completely.

For the iced cookies, roll out the fondant icing to 2 mm/¹⁄₁₆ inch thick on a sheet of baking parchment. Brush a thin layer of apricot jam over the cookies. With the cutter, stamp out hearts from the icing and use to top each of the cookies. Using the straw, make a hole in the icing above the original cookie hole, so it can be threaded. Using a soft-bristled brush, dust the cookies with gold lustre and leave to dry. You can achieve different effects by brushing on varying amounts of the lustre, or could even leave some plain white.

Thread each cookie with organza ribbon and tie in a bow, to serve.

mint chocolate kisses

This is the kind of treat to put a smile on your face — it has something to do with the nostalgic combination of chocolate, peppermint and sugar sprinkles. You could also try dipping just the top cookie in chocolate glaze and coating in sprinkles, too.

175 g/6 oz. dark/bittersweet
    chocolate, chopped
175 g/1½ sticks unsalted butter,
    softened
2 eggs
225 g/1 cup plus 2 tablespoons
    packed light muscovado/light
    brown sugar
250 g/2 cups self-raising flour
¾ teaspoon baking powder
a pinch of salt

for the minty buttercream
75 g/5 tablespoons unsalted
    butter, softened
150 g/1 cup icing/confectioners'
    sugar, sifted
½–1 teaspoon peppermint
    extract

to decorate
200 g/6½ oz. dark/bittersweet
    chocolate, chopped
sugar sprinkles

*2 baking sheets, lined with baking
    parchment*

makes 18

Put the chocolate and butter in a heatproof bowl set over a pan of barely simmering water. Stir until smooth and thoroughly combined.

Put the eggs and sugar in the bowl of a stand mixer fitted with the whisk attachment (or use an electric whisk and mixing bowl) and beat until pale and light. Add the chocolate mixture and mix until smooth.

Sift together the flour, baking powder and salt. Add to the mixing bowl and stir until smooth. Bring together into a dough, cover and refrigerate for a couple of hours.

When you are ready to start baking, preheat the oven to 180°C (350°F) Gas 4.

Remove the cookie dough from the refrigerator and pull off walnut-sized pieces. Roll into balls and arrange on the prepared baking sheets. Bake in batches on the middle shelf of the preheated oven for about 12 minutes, or until the cookies are crisp on the edges but slightly soft in the middle. Leave to cool on the baking sheets for a few minutes before transferring to a wire rack to cool completely.

To make the minty buttercream, put the butter in a large bowl and, using a stand mixer or electric hand whisk, cream until really soft. Gradually add the sifted icing/confectioners' sugar and beat until pale and smooth. Add peppermint extract to taste.

Sandwich the cold cookies together with the minty buttercream.

To decorate, put the chocolate in a heatproof bowl set over a pan of barely simmering water. Stir until smooth and melted. Leave to cool slightly, then half-dip the cookies in the melted chocolate and sprinkle with sugar sprinkles. Allow to set on a sheet of baking parchment before serving.

cherry biscotti

Crisp, citrusy biscotti studded with dried cherries and almonds make a lovely coffee–time treat. For a special occasion, they look beautiful bound together with a wide strip of decorative paper or ribbon and laid on a pretty serving plate.

2 eggs

grated zest of ½ orange

85 g/²⁄₃ cup plain/all-purpose flour

85 g/²⁄₃ cup self-raising flour

60 g/½ cup polenta/fine cornmeal

85 g/scant ½ cup caster/granulated sugar

60 g/½ cup dried cherries

60 g/½ cup blanched almonds

a baking sheet, greased

makes 20

Preheat the oven to 160°C (325°F) Gas 3.

Beat together the eggs and orange zest and set aside.

Combine the flours, polenta/cornmeal and sugar and sift together into a large mixing bowl. Make a well in the centre and pour in the egg mixture. Add the cherries and almonds and stir together to combine, then knead gently to make a soft, sticky dough.

Shape the dough into a flat log about 20 cm/8 inches long, 8 cm/3½ inches wide and 2 cm/³⁄₄ inch high and place on the prepared baking sheet. Bake in the preheated oven for about 30 minutes until golden.

Remove the log from the oven (leaving the oven on) and allow to cool on the baking sheet for about 5 minutes. Transfer the log to a chopping board and use a serrated knife to gently slice the log into 8-mm/³⁄₈-inch thick slices. Arrange the biscotti slices in a single layer on the baking sheet and bake for a further 15–20 minutes until crisp and golden. Transfer to a wire rack to cool.

lemon cookies

These lovely lemon treats are quick and easy to make. They're also great for home freezing, so it's worth baking an extra batch if you have the space.

150 g/1¼ sticks salted butter,
   firm but not hard
90 g/scant ½ cup golden
   caster/granulated sugar
170 g/1⅓ cups self-raising flour
55 g/scant ½ cup plain/
   all-purpose flour
finely grated zest of 2 lemons

a 5-cm/2-inch round cookie cutter
a baking sheet, lined with baking
  parchment

makes 18–20

Preheat the oven to 170°C (325°F) Gas 3.

In a large bowl, cream together the butter and sugar until pale and fluffy. Sift the flours into another bowl. Add a quarter of the total flours to the creamed butter and stir in. Add another quarter of the flour and the lemon zest and begin rubbing the mixture together using your fingertips. Add the remaining flour, and mix again with your fingers. Knead gently into a malleable ball of dough. (This can also be done in a food processor, blending until the ingredients form a smooth ball of dough.)

Transfer the cookie dough to a lightly floured surface and roll it out to about 1 cm/½ inch thick. Stamp out discs with the cookie cutter and arrange them 4 cm/1½ inches apart on the prepared baking sheet. Gather up and re-roll any leftover dough and cut out cookies, as before, until all the dough is used up.

Bake the cookies in the preheated oven for 20 minutes, or until the bases are golden and the tops are almost firm to the touch. Remove from the oven and leave to cool and set on the baking sheet before serving.

popcorn cookies

350 g/2⅔ cups self-raising flour
1 teaspoon bicarbonate of soda/
    baking soda
grated zest of 1 lemon
160 g/¾ cup caster/granulated
    sugar
125 g/1 stick butter
60 ml/¼ cup golden syrup/light
    corn syrup
1 egg
35 g/2½ tablespoons cream
    cheese
200 g/7 oz. white chocolate,
    chopped
100 g/¾ cup macadamia nuts,
    halved
60 g/2 oz. caramel-coated
    popcorn (such as Butterkist)

*2 baking sheets, lined with baking
parchment*

makes 16

These delicious cookies, with hints of lemon and chocolate and a crunch of popcorn, will disappear from the plate as soon as they are served. They are quite simply irresistible and are the perfect accompaniment to a glass of ice cold milk.

Preheat the oven to 180°C (350°F) Gas 4.

Sift the flour and bicarbonate of soda/baking soda into a large mixing bowl and stir in the lemon zest and sugar.

Heat the butter and syrup in a heavy-based saucepan until the butter has melted. Pour the butter over the flour and mix together with a wooden spoon. Allow to cool for a few minutes then beat in the egg and cream cheese. Stir in the chocolate chunks, macadamia nuts and popcorn and then bring the dough together with your hands.

Break off small balls of the cookie dough (about the size of a large walnut) and arrange them on the prepared baking sheets. Make sure you leave a little space between them as they will spread during cooking. Press each cookie down with your fingers, then bake in the preheated oven for 10–15 minutes until golden brown on top but still slightly soft in the middle.

Remove the cookies from the oven and allow to cool on the baking sheets for a few minutes, then transfer to a wire rack to cool completely.

gingerbread dancing shoes

Who says gingerbread should just be for Christmas? These gingerbread cookies are inspired by some rather splendid flamenco shoes. Shoe cutters come in all shapes, sizes and styles, so go for your favourites.

2 tablespoons golden syrup/light corn syrup
1 large egg yolk
200 g/1⅓ cups plain/all-purpose flour, plus extra for dusting
½ teaspoon baking powder
1½ teaspoons ground ginger
1 teaspoon ground cinnamon
¼ teaspoon freshly grated nutmeg
a pinch of salt
100 g/7 tablespoons unsalted butter, chilled and cubed
75 g/⅓ cup light muscovado/light brown sugar
plain/all-purpose flour, for rolling out

for the decoration
500 g/1 lb. royal icing sugar/mix
75–100 ml/⅓–½ cup cold water
blue and red food colouring pastes
small blue and red sugar-coated chocolate drops

a high-heeled dancing-shoe cutter (about 10–12 cm/4–5 inches long)
2 baking sheets, lined with baking parchment
disposable piping bags

makes 10–12

Beat together the golden syrup/light corn syrup and egg yolk in a small bowl.

Sift the flour, baking powder, spices and salt into a food processor and add the butter. Use the pulse button to process the mixture. When the mixture starts to look like sand and there are no lumps of butter, add the sugar and pulse again for 30 seconds to incorporate. With the motor running, add the egg-yolk mixture and pulse until starting to clump together.

Tip the mixture out onto a very lightly floured surface and knead gently to bring together into a smooth ball. Flatten the dough into a disc, wrap in clingfilm/plastic wrap and refrigerate for 1–2 hours.

Preheat the oven to 170°C (325°F) Gas 3.

Lightly dust a clean, dry surface with flour and roll out the dough evenly to a thickness of 2–3 mm/⅛ inch. Use the cutters to stamp out as many cookies as possible from the dough, cutting each one as close as possible to the next one. Arrange the cookies on the prepared baking sheets. Gather the dough scraps together, knead lightly, re-roll and stamp out more cookies until all the dough has been used up. Bake the gingerbread in batches on the middle shelf of the preheated oven for 10–12 minutes or until firm and lightly browned at the edges. Allow the cookies to cool completely on the baking sheets.

Tip the royal icing sugar/mix into a large mixing bowl and add the water gradually, mixing with a whisk until the icing is smooth and thick enough that it will hold a ribbon trail when the spoon or whisk is lifted from the bowl. This will be the consistency that you need for piping outlines or details on the cookies. You may need to add slightly more or less water to achieve the right balance.

Leave one quarter of the icing in the mixing bowl and divide the remaining icing between 2 bowls. Using the food colouring pastes, tint one bowl of icing blue and one red. Cover the bowls and set aside.

Fill the piping bag with the white icing and pipe outlines around the edge of each cookie. Leave to dry for 10 minutes.

Flood the insides of half the cookies with the reserved red icing and the other half with the blue icing and allow to dry for no more than 5 minutes. Pipe white dots onto each cookie. Embellish the shoes with sugar-coated chocolate drops. Allow the cookies to dry completely before serving.

brookies

for the cookie dough

**125 g/1 cup plain/all-purpose
flour**

**½ teaspoon bicarbonate
of soda/baking soda**

a pinch of salt

**100 g/7 tablespoons butter,
softened**

**100 g/½ cup soft light brown
sugar**

**50 g/¼ cup caster/granulated
sugar**

1 egg, lightly beaten

1 teaspoon vanilla extract

**75 g/½ cup dark/bittersweet
chocolate chips**

for the brownie mixture

**125 g/4 oz. dark/bittersweet
chocolate, chopped**

**75 g/5 tablespoons butter,
softened and cubed**

**125 g/⅔ cup caster/granulated
sugar**

2 eggs

1 teaspoon vanilla extract

60 g/½ cup plain/all-purpose flour

a pinch of salt

50 g/½ cup chopped pecans

*10 round baking pans (10 cm/
4 inches in diameter and 3 cm/
1 inch deep), greased and
baselined with baking parchment*

makes 10

*If you can't decide whether to bake brownies or cookies, why not
make both? Here, the two mixtures are combined to make one
big cookie — or is it a brownie?*

Preheat the oven to 170°C (325°F)
Gas 3.

Make the cookie dough first. Sift
together the flour, bicarbonate of soda/
baking soda and salt. In a separate bowl,
cream together the butter and sugars
until pale and light. Gradually add the
egg, beating well after each addition. Stir
in the vanilla extract. Fold the sifted
dry ingredients into the bowl until well
incorporated, then stir in the chocolate
chips. Cover the bowl and refrigerate
for 30 minutes.

Now make the brownie mixture. Put
the chocolate and butter in a heatproof
bowl set over a saucepan of barely
simmering water. Stir until both are
melted and the mixture is smooth.
Leave to cool slightly.

In a separate mixing bowl, whisk the
sugar, eggs and vanilla extract until pale

and doubled in volume. Add the melted
chocolate and butter mixture and stir
until combined. Sift the flour and salt
over the mixture and fold in until
everything is well incorporated, then
stir in the chopped pecans.

Divide the brownie mixture equally
between the prepared baking pans and
spread level. Using a spoon, roughly
dollop the cookie dough on top of the
brownie mixture.

Place the pans on a baking sheet and
bake on the middle shelf of the preheated
oven for about 15 minutes, or until the
cookie dough is golden brown.

Remove from the oven and leave to
cool in the pans for 5 minutes, then
loosen the edges of each brookie with
a small palette knife. Tip the brookies
out onto a wire rack and leave to cool
completely before serving.

petits fours brownies

Cut these into bite-size squares, top with a swirl of rich ganache and serve after dinner with coffee in place of a box of chocolates.

50 g/½ cup dried sour cherries, roughly chopped, or raisins

2 tablespoons brandy, sweet sherry (PX) or Marsala

125 g/4 oz. dark/bittersweet chocolate, chopped

75 g/5 tablespoons butter, softened

125 g/½ cup plus 2 tablespoons caster/granulated sugar

2 eggs

½ teaspoon vanilla extract

50 g/¼ cup plain/all-purpose flour

a pinch of salt

for the chocolate ganache

75 g/3 oz. dark/bittersweet chocolate, finely chopped

75 ml/5 tablespoons double/heavy cream

1 tablespoon light muscovado/light brown sugar

a pinch of salt

to decorate

crystallized roses/violets, candied ginger, candied orange peel, silver and gold dragées

a baking pan (17 cm/6½ inches square), greased and lined with greased baking parchment

a piping bag fitted with a star nozzle/tip

makes 25–36

Tip the cherries into a small saucepan, add the brandy and warm gently over low heat. Remove from the heat and leave to cool and soak for 15 minutes.

Preheat the oven to 170°C (325°F) Gas 3.

Put the chocolate and butter in a heatproof bowl set over a saucepan of barely simmering water. Stir until both are melted and the mixture is smooth. Leave to cool slightly.

Put the sugar and eggs in a mixing bowl and whisk until thick and pale. Add the vanilla and the soaked cherries with any remaining brandy. Sift the flour and salt into the bowl and fold in until well incorporated.

Pour the mixture into the prepared baking pan, spread level and bake on the middle shelf of the preheated oven for about 15 minutes. Remove from the oven and leave to cool completely in the pan, then refrigerate, still in the pan, until the brownies are firm.

Meanwhile, prepare the chocolate ganache. Put the chocolate in a small, heatproof bowl. In a small saucepan, heat the cream and sugar until the sugar has dissolved and the cream is just boiling. Add the salt, then pour it over the chopped chocolate and leave to melt. Stir until smooth, then leave to cool and thicken slightly. Spoon the ganache into the prepared piping bag.

Tip the firm brownies out of the pan onto a chopping board and cut into about 25–36 cubes. Pipe chocolate ganache rosettes onto the top of each cube. Top each ganache swirl with your choice of decoration and refrigerate until ready to serve.

very berry chocolate brownies

These brownies are a wonderful combination of fruity cheesecake on a chocolate base. They are very rich but quite delicious served as a special dessert or as mini sweet bites for a party.

for the brownie base

200 g/7 oz. dark/bittersweet chocolate, chopped
150 g/1¼ sticks unsalted butter, chilled and cubed
3 eggs
150 g/¾ cup golden caster/granulated sugar
60 g/½ cup fine rice flour*
40 g/⅓ cup ground almonds*

for the cheesecake topping

300 g/10 oz. full-fat cream cheese, at room temperature
100 g/½ cup golden caster/granulated sugar
2 eggs, beaten
½ teaspoon vanilla extract
125 g/1 cup mixed fresh berries, such as raspberries, blueberries and blackberries

a baking pan (22 cm/9 inches square), base and sides lined with a single piece of foil

makes 16 large squares or 30 mini bites

Preheat the oven to 170°C (325°F) Gas 3.

To make the brownie base, put the chocolate and butter in a heatproof bowl set over a saucepan of barely simmering water. Stir until both are melted and the mixture is smooth. Leave to cool slightly.

Beat the eggs and sugar together in a separate bowl. Fold in the rice flour and ground almonds. Add the melted chocolate mixture and gently fold it all together.

Pour the mixture into the prepared brownie pan and tap it on the work surface to ensure it is level.

To make the cheesecake topping, beat the cream cheese and sugar together in a bowl using a wooden spoon. Add the eggs and vanilla extract and mix in. (You may find it easier to use an electric hand whisk to beat the mixture to a smooth and quite runny consistency.)

Pour the cheesecake mixture over the brownie base and push it into the corners with a palette knife or the back of a metal spoon.

Push the berries into the cheesecake, covering as much or as little of the surface as you wish.

Bake in the preheated oven for about 40–45 minutes, until risen, golden and firm around the edges, but still pale in the middle and with a slight wobble.

Leave to cool in the pan for at least 2 hours, then transfer the pan to the refrigerator to chill.

Use the foil lining to lift the chilled brownies out onto a chopping board and cut into squares with a hot knife. You may want to wipe the knife clean between each cut as it will be messy and doing so will keep each brownie square looking neat.

The brownies will keep stored in an airtight container in the refrigerator for up to 4 days, but do bring them back to room temperature before eating.

* Note: if preferred you can use 100 g/ scant ½ cup of plain/all-purpose flour as an alternative to the rice flour and ground almonds.

brownie pops

Fun brownie pops are wonderful for children's parties. These are decorated with festive sprinkles, but you can let your imagination run wild and make the most of the huge assortment of sprinkles available.

100 g/1 cup shelled walnuts or pecans (optional)
200 g/7 oz. dark/bittersweet chocolate, chopped
175 g/1½ sticks butter, cubed
250 g/1¼ cups caster/granulated sugar
4 eggs
1 teaspoon vanilla extract
125 g/1 cup plain/all-purpose flour
2 tablespoons cocoa powder
a pinch of salt
75 g/½ cup milk chocolate chips
3–4 tablespoons apricot or raspberry jam/jelly

for the milk chocolate frosting
125 g/4 oz. dark/bittersweet chocolate, finely chopped (a cocoa percentage of around 54–68% is best)
125 g/4 oz. milk chocolate, finely chopped
175 ml/⅔ cup double/heavy cream
1 tablespoon maple syrup or golden syrup/light corn syrup
125 g/1 stick butter, softened and cubed

to decorate
assorted sugar sprinkles, stars and other edible festive decorations

a baking pan (20 x 30 cm/ 8 x 12 inches), greased and lined with greased baking parchment
a 5-cm/2-inch round cookie cutter
24 wooden lollipop/popsicle sticks

makes 24

It is easiest to stamp out brownie shapes if the base is prepared and baked the day before you plan to decorate your brownies.

Preheat the oven to 170°C (325°F) Gas 3.

If you're adding nuts to the brownies, tip them onto a baking sheet and lightly toast in the preheated oven for 5 minutes. Roughly chop the nuts, then leave them to cool. Leave the oven on to bake the brownies.

Put the chocolate and butter in a heatproof bowl set over a saucepan of barely simmering water. Stir until both are melted and the mixture is smooth. Leave to cool slightly.

In a separate bowl, whisk the sugar, eggs and vanilla extract with a balloon whisk until pale and thick. Add the melted chocolate mixture and stir until combined. Sift the flour, cocoa powder and salt into the bowl and fold in until well incorporated, then stir in the chocolate chips and toasted nuts (if using). Pour the mixture into the prepared baking pan, spread level and bake on the middle shelf of the preheated oven for 25 minutes. Remove the brownies from the oven and leave to cool completely in the pan.

Remove the cold brownie from the pan. Using the cookie cutter, stamp out 24 rounds from the brownies and arrange on a board or tray.

Warm the jam in a small saucepan, sieve/strain it, then brush it all over the brownie rounds. Leave on a wire rack for 5–10 minutes to set.

To prepare the milk chocolate frosting, tip the chocolates into a small, heatproof bowl. Heat the cream and syrup in a small saucepan until only just boiling. Pour it over the chopped chocolates, add the butter and leave to melt. Stir until smooth, then leave to thicken slightly.

Using a palette knife, spread the frosting evenly all over the brownie rounds, then push a lollipop/popsicle stick into each pop. Lay them on a sheet of baking parchment and leave until the frosting is starting to set. Decorate with an assortment of sprinkles and festive decorations by making patterns on the faces of the pops and by scattering sprinkles generously over the edges.

cherry & coconut brownies

Dried cherries, coconut and rich chocolate are a marriage made in choccy heaven. Top each square with toasted fresh coconut shavings and the finest cherries.

200 g/7 oz. dark/bittersweet chocolate, chopped
125 g/1 stick butter, softened and cubed
200 g/1 cup caster/granulated sugar
4 eggs
75 g/²⁄₃ cup plain/all-purpose flour
a pinch of salt
75 g/2½ oz. natural glacé/candied cherries, roughly chopped
50 g/½ cup dried sour cherries, roughly chopped
50 g/²⁄₃ cup desiccated/dried shredded coconut

for the chocolate ganache
150 g/5½ oz. dark/bittersweet chocolate, finely chopped
150 ml/²⁄₃ cup double/heavy cream
1 tablespoon light muscovado/light brown sugar
a pinch of salt

to decorate
fresh coconut shavings, toasted
16 fresh cherries, stems intact

a baking pan (23 cm/9 inches square), greased and lined with greased baking parchment

makes 16 squares

Preheat the oven to 170°C (325°F) Gas 3.

Put the chocolate and butter in a heatproof bowl set over a saucepan of barely simmering water. Stir until both are melted and the mixture is smooth. Leave to cool slightly.

In a separate bowl, lightly whisk the sugar and eggs with a balloon whisk for 1–2 minutes. Add the melted chocolate mixture and stir until combined. Sift the flour and salt into the bowl and fold in until well incorporated, then stir in the glacé/candied cherries, sour cherries and coconut.

Pour the mixture into the prepared baking pan, spread level and bake on the middle shelf of the preheated oven for about 20–25 minutes. Remove the brownies from the oven and leave to cool completely in the pan.

Meanwhile, prepare the chocolate ganache. Tip the chocolate into a small, heatproof bowl. Heat the cream and sugar in a small saucepan until the sugar has dissolved and the cream is just boiling. Add the salt. Pour it over the chopped chocolate and leave to melt. Stir until smooth, then leave to cool and thicken slightly.

Cut the cold brownies into 16 squares. Spread a tablespoonful of the ganache over each square and top with coconut shavings and a fresh cherry.

coffee blondies

Use a vegetable peeler to make piles of chocolate shavings for decorating these cappuccino-like squares.

100 g/1 cup shelled pecans

200 g/1 cup light muscovado/ light brown sugar

175 g/1½ sticks butter

3 tablespoons instant coffee granules

2 eggs, lightly beaten

1 teaspoon vanilla extract

250 g/2 cups plain/all-purpose flour

2 teaspoons baking powder

a pinch of salt

100 g/⅔ cup dark/bittersweet chocolate chips

to decorate

200 ml/¾ cup double/heavy cream

2 tablespoons icing/ confectioners' sugar

mixed chocolate shavings

chocolate-coated coffee beans

a baking pan (20 x 30 cm/8 x 12 inches), greased and lined with greased baking parchment

makes 16–20

Preheat the oven to 170°C (325°F) Gas 3.

Tip the pecans onto a baking sheet and lightly toast in the preheated oven for 5 minutes. Roughly chop the pecans, then leave them to cool. Leave the oven on to bake the brownies.

Tip the muscovado/brown sugar and butter into a saucepan set over low–medium heat and melt, stirring constantly. In a small bowl, dissolve the coffee granules in 1½ tablespoons boiling water. Stir two-thirds into the pan (reserve the rest for the frosting). Remove from the heat, transfer the mixture to a heatproof bowl and leave to cool completely.

Stir the eggs and vanilla extract into the bowl until smooth. Sift the flour, baking powder and salt into the bowl and fold in until well mixed, then stir in the chocolate chips and pecans.

Pour the mixture into the prepared baking pan, spread level and bake on the middle shelf of the preheated oven for about 25 minutes, or until just set in the middle and the top has formed a light crust. Remove from the oven and leave to cool completely in the pan.

To decorate, whip the cream with the icing/confectioners' sugar and the reserved coffee.

Turn the brownie out of the pan onto a chopping board and cut into portions. Top each brownie with a dollop of coffee cream, then scatter chocolate shavings and coffee beans over the top, to finish.

doughnuts & whoopie pies

Whether your favourite is a traditional jam doughnut, oozing with sweet fruit at every bite, or a classic glazed doughnut topped with cheerful sprinkles, this selection of irresistible treats will satisfy the sweetest of tooths. While naughty coconut doughnuts are spiked with rum, the pistachio doughnuts are bursting with a scrumptious nutty filling. Or go for a whoopie pie; not quite a cake, not quite a cookie, there is something about these delightfully squidgy treats that just makes people smile. Sandwiched together with creamy fillings such as peanut butter and jelly, amaretto cream or simply ice cream, whip up a batch today and spread a little happiness to those you love.

traditional jam doughnuts

200 ml/¾ cup warm milk
7 g/¼ oz. fast-action dried yeast
30 g/2½ tablespoons caster/
 granulated sugar
300 g/2⅓ cups plain/all-purpose
 flour, plus extra for dusting
160 g/1¼ cups strong white
 bread flour
½ teaspoon salt
2 eggs, beaten
60 g/½ stick butter, softened
sunflower oil, for greasing
 and frying
caster/superfine sugar,
 for dusting
450 g/16 oz. strawberry
 or raspberry jam/jelly

*16 small squares of baking parchment
a piping bag fitted with a round
 nozzle/tip*

makes 16

A jam doughnut is the classic — dusted in sugar and oozing with strawberry or raspberry jam when you bite into the middle. It is always best to serve these doughnuts fresh and make sure that you fill them generously — there is nothing worse than a meanly-filled doughnut! By turning them over halfway through cooking, you should end up with the classic white line around the perimeter of the doughnut.

Whisk together the warm milk, yeast and sugar in a jug/pitcher and leave in a warm place for about 10 minutes until a thick foam has formed on top of the milk.

Meanwhile, sift the flours into a large mixing bowl, add the salt, eggs and butter and stir together, then pour in the yeast mixture. Using a stand mixer fitted with a dough hook, mix the dough on a slow speed for 2 minutes, then increase the speed and knead for about 8 minutes until the dough is soft and pliable. Alternatively, knead the dough by hand for 15 minutes. The mixture will be very soft but should not be sticky, so dust with flour if needed.

Lay the squares of baking parchment on a tray and lightly dust with flour. Divide the dough into 16 portions and, dusting your hands with flour, shape each portion into a ball and place one on each square of parchment. Cover the doughnuts with a clean damp tea/dish towel and leave to rest for 10 minutes. Reshape the balls, then leave to rise in

a warm place for about 35–45 minutes, covered in lightly-greased clingfilm/plastic wrap, until the dough has doubled in size and holds an indent when you press with a fingertip. Rest again, uncovered, for 10 minutes.

In a large saucepan or deep fat fryer, heat the oil to 190°C (375°F). Holding the square of parchment, transfer each doughnut to the pan, one at a time, being careful not to handle the dough or splash hot oil. Cook in small batches for about 1½ minutes on each side until golden brown. Remove the doughnuts from the oil using a slotted spoon and drain on paper towels.

When the doughnuts are cool enough to handle, pour the dusting sugar into a shallow dish and roll each doughnut in the sugar to coat thoroughly. Use a round teaspoon handle to poke a hole in the doughnut and move it around to make a cavity inside. Spoon the jam/jelly into the piping bag and pipe into the cavity in each doughnut and serve.

glazed sprinkle doughnuts

200 ml/¾ cup warm milk

7 g/¼ oz. fast-action dried yeast

30 g/2½ tablespoons caster/
   granulated sugar

300 g/2⅓ cups plain/all-purpose
   flour, plus extra for dusting

160 g/1¼ cups strong white
   bread flour

½ teaspoon salt

2 eggs, beaten

60 g/½ stick butter, softened

1 teaspoon vanilla extract

sunflower oil, for greasing
   and frying

to decorate

225 g/1½ cups icing/
   confectioners' sugar

pink food colouring (optional)

sugar sprinkles, to decorate

18 small squares of baking parchment
a 2-cm/¾-inch round cookie cutter

makes 18

These delicious glazed vanilla doughnuts, decorated with cheerfully-coloured sprinkles, are unbeatable for those who prefer to keep things simple.

Whisk together the warm milk, yeast and sugar in a jug/pitcher and leave in a warm place for about 10 minutes until a thick foam has formed on top of the milk.

Meanwhile, sift the flours into a large mixing bowl, add the salt, eggs, butter and vanilla and stir together, then pour in the yeast mixture. Using a stand mixer fitted with a dough hook, mix the dough on a slow speed for 2 minutes, then increase the speed and knead for about 8 minutes until the dough is soft and pliable. Alternatively, knead the dough by hand for 15 minutes. The mixture will be very soft but should not be sticky, so dust with flour if needed.

Lay the squares of baking parchment on a tray and lightly dust with flour. Divide the dough into 16 portions and, dusting your hands with flour, roll into balls. Using the cookie cutter, cut out a hole from the centre of each dough ball to create a ring. Place each ring on a square of baking parchment. Combine the cut-out dough and mould into balls to make further rings – you should be able to make 18 in total. Cover the doughnuts with a clean damp tea/dish towel and leave to rest for 10 minutes, and then leave to rise in a warm place for

about 35–45 minutes, covered in lightly-greased clingfilm/plastic wrap, until the dough has doubled in size and holds an indent when you press with a fingertip. Rest again, uncovered, for 10 minutes.

In a large saucepan or deep fat fryer, heat the oil to 190°C (375°F). Holding the square of parchment, transfer each doughnut to the pan, one at a time, being careful not to handle the dough or splash hot oil. Cook in small batches for about 1½ minutes on each side until golden brown. Remove the doughnuts from the oil using a slotted spoon and drain on paper towels, then leave them to cool on a wire rack. Slide a sheet of foil under the rack to catch any drips of glaze later on.

Mix together the confectioners'/icing sugar, 80 ml/⅓ cup water and the food colouring, if using, to form a smooth thin glaze. Dip the top of each doughnut into the glaze to coat and scatter over the sugar sprinkles while the glaze is still sticky (it is best to do this in small batches as the glaze can dry quickly). Leave the icing to set before serving.

lemon ring doughnuts

200 ml/¾ cup warm milk
7 g/¼ oz. fast-action dried yeast
30 g/2½ tablespoons caster/
    granulated sugar
300 g/2⅓ cups plain/all-purpose
    flour, plus extra for dusting
160 g/1¼ cups strong white
    bread flour
½ teaspoon salt
2 eggs, beaten
60 g/½ stick butter, softened
grated zest of 2 lemons
sunflower oil, for greasing
    and frying
sugar sprinkles, to decorate

for the dipping glaze
freshly squeezed juice of
    3 lemons
150 g/1 cup icing/confectioners'
    sugar, sifted

to decorate
85 g/⅔ cup icing/confectioners'
    sugar, sifted
freshly squeezed juice of 1 lemon
yellow food colouring

18 small squares of baking
    parchment
a 2-cm/¾-inch round cookie cutter
a piping bag fitted with a small round
    nozzle/tip

makes 18

These zingy doughnuts, bursting with lemon, are a tasty treat. Drizzled with a tangy lemon glaze and decorated with sugar sprinkles, they look almost too pretty to eat. If you want to try making orange doughnuts, simply substitute orange zest and juice in place of the lemon.

Whisk together the warm milk, yeast and sugar in a jug/pitcher and leave in a warm place for about 10 minutes until a thick foam has formed on top of the milk.

Meanwhile, sift the flours into a large mixing bowl, add the salt, eggs, butter and lemon zest and stir together, then pour in the yeast mixture. Using a stand mixer fitted with a dough hook, mix the dough on a slow speed for 2 minutes, then increase the speed and knead for about 8 minutes until the dough is soft and pliable. Alternatively, knead the dough by hand. The mixture will be very soft but should not be sticky, so dust with flour if needed.

Lay the squares of baking parchment on a tray and lightly dust with flour. Divide the dough into 16 portions and, dusting your hands with flour, roll into balls. Using the cookie cutter, cut out a hole from the centre of each dough ball to create a ring. Place each ring on a square of baking parchment. Combine the cut-out dough and mould into balls to make further rings – you should be able to make 18 in total. Cover the rings with a clean damp tea/dish towel and leave to rest for 10 minutes, and then let rise in a warm place for about 35–45 minutes, covered in lightly-greased clingfilm/plastic wrap, until the dough has doubled in size and holds an indent when you press

with a fingertip. Rest again, uncovered, for 10 minutes.

In a large saucepan or deep fat fryer, heat the oil to 190°C (375°F). Holding the square of parchment, transfer each doughnut to the pan, one at a time, being careful not to handle the dough or splash hot oil. Cook in small batches for about 1½ minutes on each side until golden brown. Remove the doughnuts from the oil using a slotted spoon and drain on paper towels, then let cool on a wire rack. Slide a sheet of foil under the rack to catch any drips of glaze later on.

For the dipping glaze, put the lemon juice and icing/confectioners' sugar in a saucepan set over medium heat, stir and simmer for 3–5 minutes until syrupy. Remove from the heat and, one at a time, dip each doughnut in the syrup to coat completely. Remove with a slotted spoon and transfer to the wire rack to set.

To prepare the frosting, put the icing/confectioners' sugar in a bowl and add the lemon juice gradually (you may not need it all), along with a few drops of food colouring, stirring until you have a smooth thick frosting. Spoon into a piping bag and pipe drizzles on top of the doughnut, then decorate with sugar sprinkles. Leave to set before serving.

coconut doughnuts

Coconut rum and fluffy shredded coconut make a tropical topping for these light doughnuts. They are baked in the oven rather than fried, so are not quite so naughty. Decorate in pink and white for a fun twist inspired by retro coconut ice candy!

300 g/2⅓ cups self-raising flour
1 teaspoon baking powder
85 g/scant ½ cup soft light
   brown sugar
½ teaspoon salt
2 eggs, beaten
50 g/3 tablespoons butter,
   softened
250 ml/1 cup milk
1 tablespoon coconut rum

for the coconut glaze
400 g/2⅔ cups icing/
   confectioners' sugar, sifted
130 ml/½ cup coconut milk
1 tablespoon coconut rum

to decorate
80 g/1½ cup soft shredded
   coconut
pink food colouring

*3 x 6-hole doughnut pans, greased
a piping bag fitted with a large
   round nozzle/tip*

makes 18

Preheat the oven to 180°C (350°F) Gas 4.

Sift the flour into a large mixing bowl. Add all the remaining doughnut ingredients and beat to a smooth batter with a stand mixer or electric hand whisk. Spoon the mixture into the prepared doughnut pans. This is easiest done by transferring the batter to a piping bag and piping it into each hole. Bake the doughnuts in the preheated oven for 10–15 minutes or until golden brown. (If you don't have three doughnut pans, you can bake them in batches, washing the pan between each batch.) Remove from the oven and turn the doughnuts out onto a wire rack to cool. Slide a sheet of foil under the rack to catch any drips of glaze later on.

Divide the shredded coconut equally between two bowls. Using a few drops of food colouring, tint half of the coconut pink and leave the remaining half white.

For the coconut glaze, put the icing/confectioners' sugar, coconut milk and rum in a saucepan set over medium heat and simmer for 3–5 minutes until the liquid reduces slightly and becomes syrupy. Remove from the heat and, one at a time, dip each doughnut in the syrup to coat completely. Remove with a slotted spoon and transfer to the wire rack. Sprinkle over the shredded coconut while the glaze is still sticky, coating half of the doughnuts with pink coconut and half with white. Leave to set before serving.

raspberry ring doughnuts

These dainty doughnuts are bursting with a sharp raspberry flavour. The frosting is made with fresh raspberry juice rather than food colouring, which gives a vibrant colour as well as adding extra flavour. They are topped with fresh raspberries and red edible glitter, but you could decorate simply with sprinkles or dried raspberry pieces, if you prefer.

300 g/2⅓ cups self-raising flour
1 teaspoon baking powder
70 g/⅓ cup caster/granulated
   sugar
½ teaspoon salt
2 eggs, beaten
50 g/3 tablespoons butter,
   softened
250 ml/1 cup raspberry yogurt
1 teaspoon almond extract
fresh raspberries, to decorate
red edible glitter, to decorate
   (optional)

for the frosting
100 g/1½ cups fresh raspberries
300 g/2 cups icing/confectioners'
   sugar, sifted

*3 x 12-hole mini doughnut pans,
   greased*

makes 36

Preheat the oven to 180°C (350°F) Gas 4.

Sift the flour into a large mixing bowl. Add all the remaining doughnut ingredients (except the raspberries and glitter) and beat to a smooth batter with a stand mixer or electric hand whisk. Spoon the mixture into the prepared doughnut pans. This is easiest done by transferring the batter to a piping bag and piping it into each hole. Bake in the preheated oven for 10–15 minutes until the doughnuts are golden brown. (If you don't have three doughnut pans, you can bake them in batches, washing the pan between each batch.) Remove from the oven and turn the doughnuts out onto a wire rack to cool. Slide a sheet of foil under the rack to catch any drips of glaze later on.

To make the frosting, put the raspberries in a fine mesh sieve/strainer set over a bowl and use the back of a spoon to push them through the mesh to release their juice. Discard the seeds. Put the icing/confectioners' sugar into a small mixing bowl and add the raspberry juice gradually (you may not need it all), stirring until you have a smooth thick frosting. Spread a layer of frosting over the top of each doughnut using a round-bladed knife and decorate with a whole raspberry. Sprinkle over the edible glitter, if using, then return to the wire rack for the frosting to set completely before serving.

yum yums

These classic American doughnut twists are made with a yeast dough, which is folded to create air pockets and makes these doughnuts really light.

200 ml/¾ cup warm milk

7 g/¼ oz. fast-action dried yeast

30 g/2½ tablespoons caster/
  granulated sugar

300 g/2⅓ cups plain/all-purpose
  flour, plus extra for dusting

160 g/1¼ cups strong white
  bread flour

½ teaspoon salt

2 eggs

1 teaspoon vanilla extract

110 g/7 tablespoons butter,
  softened

sunflower oil, for greasing
  and frying

for the glaze

250 g/2 cups icing/confectioners'
  sugar, sifted

1 teaspoon vanilla extract

*14 small rectangles of baking
  parchment*

makes 14

Whisk together the warm milk, yeast and sugar in a jug/pitcher and leave in a warm place for about 10 minutes until a thick foam has formed on top of the milk.

Meanwhile, sift the flours into a large mixing bowl, add the salt, eggs, vanilla and 60 g/4 tablespoons of the butter and stir together, then pour in the yeast mixture. Using a stand mixer fitted with a dough hook, mix the dough on a slow speed for 2 minutes, then increase the speed and knead for about 8 minutes until the dough is soft and pliable. Alternatively, knead the dough by hand for 15 minutes. The mixture will be very soft but should not be sticky, so dust with flour if needed.

Leave the dough to rest for 10 minutes, then roll out on a flour-dusted surface to form a rectangle measuring 25 x 35 cm/ 10 x 14 inches. Spread the remaining butter gently over the dough using your finger tips. With the shortest edge of the rectangle toward you, fold the bottom third up. Turn the dough 180°, and again fold the bottom third up so that it rests on top of the first fold and all the butter is inside the dough. Leave to rest for 10 minutes covered by a clean damp tea/dish towel. Roll out the dough again, to the same size, and fold the thirds in the same way. Rest again, covered, for 10 minutes. Roll out the dough for a final time to a 30 x 40-cm/12 x 16-inch

rectangle but this time fold the two outside edges into the centre of the dough so that they meet in the middle, then fold the dough in half again so that the middle join is hidden inside the dough. Cut the dough into 14 slices and then, holding each one at the unopened end, twist the two open ends around each other to make the classic yum yum shape. Lay the rectangles of baking parchment on a tray and dust with flour. Place one twist on each piece of parchment and leave to rise in a warm place for about 35–45 minutes, covered in lightly-greased clingfilm/plastic wrap, until the dough has doubled in size. Rest again, uncovered, for 10 minutes.

In a large saucepan or deep fat fryer, heat the oil to 190°C (375°F). Holding the square of parchment, transfer each yum yum to the pan, one at a time, being careful not to handle the dough or splash hot oil. Cook in small batches for about 1½ minutes on each side until golden brown. Remove the yum yums from the oil using a slotted spoon and drain on paper towels. Leave to cool on a wire rack. Slide a sheet of foil under the rack to catch any drips of glaze later on.

Put the glaze ingredients in a saucepan with 3–4 tablespoons water and heat, stirring, until thin and syrupy. Spoon the glaze over the yum yums and leave to set before serving.

pistachio doughnuts

200 ml/¾ cup warm milk
7 g/¼ oz. fast-action dried yeast
30 g/2½ tablespoons caster/
    granulated sugar
300 g/2⅓ cups plain/all-purpose
    flour, plus extra for dusting
160 g/1¼ cups strong white
    bread flour
½ teaspoon salt
2 eggs, beaten
60 g/½ stick butter, softened
60 g/½ cup shelled and finely
    chopped pistachios
sunflower oil, for greasing
    and frying

for the pistachio cream
30 g/2 tablespoons butter,
    softened
60 g/½ cup shelled pistachios
60 g/½ cup icing/confectioners'
    sugar, sifted
300 ml/1¼ cups double/heavy
    cream

for the pistachio sugar
60 g/½ cup shelled pistachios
150 g/⅔ cup caster/superfine
    sugar

*26 small squares of baking
    parchment*
*a 4-cm/1½-inch triangular cookie
    cutter*
*a piping bag fitted with a round
    nozzle/tip*

makes 26

These doughnuts may look fairly classic from the outside but inside they are bursting with a delicious pistachio cream. They are made using a triangular cutter, but you could use any shaped cutter of your choice. Roll in sugar and pistachio crumb for a pretty effect.

Whisk together the warm milk, yeast and sugar in a jug/pitcher and leave in a warm place for about 10 minutes until a thick foam has formed on top of the milk.

Meanwhile, sift the flours into a large mixing bowl, add the salt, eggs, butter and chopped pistachios and stir together, then pour in the yeast mixture. Using a stand mixer fitted with a dough hook, mix the dough on a slow speed for 2 minutes, then increase the speed and knead for about 8 minutes until the dough is soft and pliable. Alternatively, knead the dough by hand for 15 minutes. The mixture will be very soft but should not be sticky, so dust with flour if needed.

Lay the squares of baking parchment on a tray and lightly dust with flour. Roll out the dough to 3 cm/1¼ inch thickness and cut out 26 triangles, re-modelling the dough scraps if necessary. Place each triangle on a square of baking parchment. Cover the doughnuts with a clean damp tea/dish towel and leave to rest for 10 minutes. Reshape the triangles and then leave to rise in a warm place for about 35–45 minutes, covered in lightly-greased clingfilm/plastic wrap, until the dough has doubled in size and holds an indent when you press with a fingertip. Rest again, uncovered, for 10 minutes.

In a large saucepan or deep fat fryer, heat the oil to 190°C (375°F). Holding the square of parchment, transfer each doughnut to the pan, one at a time, being careful not to handle the dough or splash hot oil. Cook in small batches for about 1½ minutes on each side until golden brown. Remove the doughnuts from the oil using a slotted spoon and drain on paper towels.

To make the pistachio sugar, blitz the pistachios to a fine dust in a food processor. Add the sugar and blend again briefly to combine, then transfer to a shallow dish. Whilst they are still warm, roll each doughnut in the pistachio sugar to coat thoroughly. Use a round teaspoon handle to poke a hole in the doughnut and move it around to make a cavity inside.

For the pistachio cream, blitz the butter, pistachios and icing/confectioners' sugar to a smooth paste in a food processor. With an electric hand whisk, whip the cream until it almost holds stiff peaks, then add the pistachio paste and whisk again until the cream is stiff. Spoon the cream into a piping bag and pipe into the centre of each doughnut. Serve or store the doughnuts in the refrigerator if not eating straight away.

vanilla whoopie pies

125 g/1 stick unsalted butter,
   softened
200 g/1 cup caster/granulated
   sugar
1 large egg
1 teaspoon vanilla extract
320 g/2½ cups self-raising flour
1 teaspoon baking powder
½ teaspoon salt
125 ml/½ cup buttermilk
125 ml/½ cup sour cream
100 ml/⅓ cup hot (not boiling)
   water

for the vanilla buttercream
90 g/6 tablespoons unsalted
   butter, softened
375 g/3 cups icing/confectioners'
   sugar, sifted
1 teaspoon vanilla extract
3 tablespoons milk
4 tablespoons raspberry jam/jelly
icing/confectioners' sugar, to dust

*2 x 12-hole whoopie pie pans,
   greased*
*a piping bag fitted with a large
   star nozzle/tip (optional)*

makes 12

Victoria sandwich cake is an English classic and much-loved teatime treat. Here, light and fluffy vanilla sponge cakes are filled with a delicate buttercream and raspberry preserve to make dainty little whoopie pies that are just perfect.

Preheat the oven to 180°C (350°F) Gas 4.

To make the pies, cream together the butter and sugar in a large mixing bowl for 2–3 minutes using an electric hand whisk, until light and fluffy. Add the egg and vanilla extract and mix again. Sift the flour and baking powder into the bowl and add the salt, buttermilk and sour cream. Whisk again until everything is well incorporated, then add the hot water and whisk into the mixture.

Put a large spoonful of mixture into each hole in the prepared whoopie pie pans. Leave to stand for 10 minutes, then bake the pies in the preheated oven for

10–12 minutes. Remove the pies from the oven, leave to cool slightly, then turn out onto a wire rack to cool completely.

To make the vanilla buttercream, whisk the butter, icing/confectioners' sugar, vanilla extract and milk together in a mixing bowl for 2–3 minutes, until light and creamy. Spoon the buttercream into the prepared piping bag and pipe a swirl of filling onto 12 of the whoopie pie halves. (If you do not have a piping bag, spread the filling over the pie halves with a round-bladed knife.) Put a teaspoon of raspberry jam on top of the buttercream. Top with the remaining pie halves and dust liberally with icing/confectioners sugar, to serve.

peanut butter & jelly pies

Peanut butter and jelly sandwiches are an all-time American classic — the saltiness of peanuts and sweetness of the jam providing the ultimate sweet and savoury combination.

125 g/1 stick unsalted butter, softened

1 tablespoon smooth peanut butter

200 g/1 cup caster/granulated sugar

1 large egg

320 g/2⅓ cups self-raising flour

1 teaspoon baking powder

½ teaspoon salt

250 ml/1 cup buttermilk

100 ml/⅓ cup hot (not boiling) water

for the peanut glaze

1 tablespoon unsalted butter

1 tablespoon smooth peanut butter

150 g/1¼ cups icing/confectioners' sugar

50 g/⅓ cup salted peanuts, chopped

for the filling

70 g/5 tablespoons unsalted butter, softened

2 tablespoons smooth peanut butter

200 g/1⅔ cups icing/confectioners' sugar, sifted

3 tablespoons sour cream

3 tablespoons raspberry jam/jelly

2 x 12-hole whoopie pie pans, greased

a piping bag fitted with a large star nozzle/tip (optional)

makes 12

Preheat the oven to 180°C (350°F) Gas 4.

To make the pies, cream together the butter, peanut butter and sugar in a large mixing bowl for 2–3 minutes using an electric hand whisk, until light and creamy. Add the egg and mix again. Sift the flour and baking powder into the bowl and add the salt and buttermilk. Whisk again until everything is well incorporated. Add the hot water and whisk into the mixture.

Put a large spoonful of mixture into each hole in the prepared whoopie pie pans. Leave to stand for 10 minutes then bake the pies in the preheated oven for 10–12 minutes. Remove the pies from the oven, leave to cool slightly, then turn out onto a wire rack.

To make the peanut glaze, heat the butter, peanut butter, icing/confectioners' sugar and 60 ml/¼ cup cold water in a saucepan set over low heat. Simmer until you have a smooth thick glaze, then spoon this over half of the pie halves. This is best done whilst the pies are still warm on the wire rack and with kitchen foil underneath to catch any drips. Leave to cool completely.

To make the filling, whisk together the butter, peanut butter, icing/confectioners' sugar and sour cream in a mixing bowl using an electric hand whisk, until light and creamy. Spoon the filling into the prepared piping bag and pipe stars of filling in a ring onto the 12 unglazed pie halves – reserving a little to decorate. (If you do not have a piping bag, thickly spread the filling over the pie halves with a round-bladed knife.) Put a spoonful of jam/jelly on top of the filling and top with the glazed pie halves. Pipe a star of the reserved filling on top of each pie and sprinkle with the chopped peanuts, to decorate.

rose & violet cream pies

These whoopie pies take all the elements of the classic rose and violet cream chocolates — their floral fondant fillings, rich dark chocolate shells and crystallized petal decorations — and transfer them to dainty little bakes that make the most elegant of teatime treats or the perfect edible gift.

125 g/1 stick unsalted butter, softened
200 g/1 cup soft dark brown sugar
1 large egg
1 teaspoon vanilla extract
280 g/2 cups plus 2 tablespoons self-raising flour
40 g/⅓ cup cocoa powder
1 teaspoon baking powder
½ teaspoon salt
250 ml/1 cup buttermilk
100 ml/⅓ cup hot (not boiling) water

for the rose and violet fillings
250 ml/1 cup double/heavy cream
250 g/1 cup mascarpone cheese
2 tablespoons icing/confectioners' sugar
1 tablespoon rose syrup
1 tablespoon violet syrup
pink and purple food colourings

to decorate
150 g/5½ oz. dark/bittersweet chocolate
crystallized rose and violet petals

2 baking sheets, lined with baking parchment or silicone mats
a piping bag fitted with a large round nozzle/tip (optional)
2 piping bags fitted with medium round nozzles/tips
24 foil petits fours cases

makes 24

Preheat the oven to 180°C (350°F) Gas 4.

To make the pies, cream together the butter and brown sugar in a large mixing bowl for 2–3 minutes using an electric hand whisk, until light and creamy. Add the egg and vanilla extract and mix again. Sift the flour, cocoa and baking powder into the bowl and add the salt and buttermilk. Whisk again until everything is well incorporated. Add the hot water and whisk into the mixture.

Spoon the mixture into the first prepared piping bag and pipe 48 rounds onto the prepared baking sheets (about 3-cm/1¼-inches diameter) leaving a gap between each pie as they will spread during baking. (Alternatively, use 2 teaspoons to form small rounds on the sheets.) Leave to stand for 10 minutes then bake each sheet in the preheated oven for 10–12 minutes. Remove the pies from the oven, leave to cool slightly, then transfer to a wire rack to cool.

To make the fillings, whip the cream to stiff peaks. In a separate bowl, beat the mascarpone until softened then fold it into the whipped cream along with the icing/confectioners' sugar. Transfer half of the mixture to a separate bowl; add the rose syrup and a few drops of pink food colouring to one bowl and the violet syrup and a drop of purple food colouring to the other. Mix both creams well with an electric hand whisk.

Spoon the fillings into the remaining prepared piping bags and pipe circles of each flavour onto 12 pie halves, so that you have 24 pie halves covered with cream. Top with the remaining pie halves.

To decorate, melt the chocolate in a heatproof bowl set over a pan of barely simmering water. Spoon a little melted chocolate onto each pie, top with a crystallized rose or violet petal, as appropriate to the filling, and allow to set. Put them in petits fours cases and your whoopie pies are ready to enjoy.

almond & amaretto pies

125 g/1 stick unsalted butter, softened

200 g/1 cup dark soft brown sugar

1 egg

1 teaspoon almond essence

280 g/2 cups plus 2 tablespoons self-raising flour

1 teaspoon baking powder

80 g/½ cup ground almonds

½ teaspoon salt

250 ml/1 cup sour cream

1 tablespoon amaretto liqueur

100 ml/⅓ cup hot (not boiling) water

for the amaretto cream

300 ml/1¼ cups double/heavy cream

50 ml/3 tablespoons amaretto liqueur

for the filling

150 g/5½ oz. white chocolate

6–7 amaretti biscuits/cookies, crumbled

2 x 12-hole whoopie pie pans, greased

a piping bag fitted with a large star nozzle/tip (optional)

makes 12

Amaretto is an Italian liqueur made from apricot kernels. These whoopie pies pay homage to this delicious drink with a delicate almond flavour and a crisp amaretti biscuit and white chocolate coating. Serve with a glass of amaretto on ice for a special treat.

Preheat the oven to 180°C (350°F) Gas 4.

To make the pies, cream together the butter and brown sugar in a large mixing bowl for 2–3 minutes using an electric hand whisk, until light and creamy. Add the egg and almond essence and mix again. Sift the flour and baking powder into the bowl and add the ground almonds, salt, sour cream and amaretto. Whisk again until everything is well incorporated. Add the hot water and whisk into the mixture.

Put a large spoonful of mixture into each hole of the prepared whoopie pie pans. Leave to stand for 10 minutes, then bake the pies in the preheated oven for 10–12 minutes. Remove the pies from the oven, leave to cool slightly, then turn out onto a wire rack to cool completely.

To decorate, melt the white chocolate in a heatproof bowl set over a pan of barely simmering water.

Sprinkle the amaretti crumbs over a plate and pour the melted chocolate into a shallow dish. Roll the sides of all the pie halves in the chocolate and then roll again in the amaretti crumbs. Return to the wire rack to set. Using a fork, drizzle the tops of 12 of the pie halves with the leftover white chocolate.

To make the amaretto cream filling, put the cream and amaretto liqueuer in a mixing bowl and whip to stiff peaks. Spoon into the prepared piping bag and pipe stars of filling onto the 12 pie halves that are not decorated with chocolate on top. (If you do not have a piping bag, spread the filling over the pie halves with a round-bladed knife.) Top with the decorated pie halves and serve.

ice cream whoopie pies

These pies are a classic chocolate whoopie, just a little bit chillier, and perfect for a barbecue party on a summer's day. You'll need to assemble them at the last minute so that the ice cream doesn't melt. Vanilla is used here, but you could substitute any flavour you like — why not try chocolate for a double chocolate treat!

125 g/1 stick unsalted butter, softened
200 g/1 cup soft dark brown sugar
1 large egg
1 teaspoon vanilla extract
280 g/2 cups plus 2 tablespoons self-raising flour
40 g/⅓ cup cocoa powder
1 teaspoon baking powder
½ teaspoon salt
250 ml/1 cup plain yogurt
100 ml/⅓ cup hot (not boiling) water

for the ice cream filling
400 g/14 oz. vanilla ice cream in a block
multicoloured sprinkles, to decorate

2 x 12-hole whoopie pie pans, greased
an 8-cm/3-inch round cookie cutter

makes 12

Preheat the oven to 180°C (350°F) Gas 4.

To make the pies, cream together the butter and brown sugar in a large mixing bowl for 2–3 minutes using an electric hand whisk until light and creamy. Add the egg and vanilla extract and mix again. Sift the flour, cocoa and baking powder into the bowl and add the salt and yogurt. Whisk again until everything is incorporated. Add the hot water and whisk into the mixture.

Put a large spoonful of mixture into each hole in the prepared whoopie pie pans. Leave to stand for 10 minutes then bake the pies in the preheated oven for 10–12 minutes. Remove the pies from the oven, leave to cool slightly, then turn out onto a wire rack to cool completely.

Shortly before you are ready to serve, remove the ice cream from the freezer and allow to soften slightly. Cut 12 slices each about 2 cm/1 inch thick and, using the cookie cutter, stamp out a round from each slice. Sandwich an ice cream round between 2 cooled pie halves.

Working quickly, put the sprinkles on a flat plate and roll the edges of each pie in them so that the ice cream is coated. Serve your whoopie pies immediately with napkins to catch any ice cream drips.

tartlets & pastries

Tiny tartlets and pastries have a truly Parisian feel. From classic Paris brest to baby éclairs, rose petal religieuses to blackcurrant millefeuilles, here you will find the daintiest of pâtisserie for every occasion. Buttery, melt-in-the mouth tartlets include richly dark and decadent salted caramel tartlets along with tangy lemon and lime meringue pies and little maids of honour. Serve up a selection for a sophisticated afternoon tea or a party spread of sweet canapés, or team up three of your favourites for a trendy trio of desserts. Whatever the occasion, these beautiful and delicious treats are guaranteed to be greeted with delight.

baby éclairs

Eclairs, traditionally topped with chocolate and filled with cream, are one of those 'naughty but nice' indulgences. These bite-size éclairs, topped with chocolate, peppermint, or coffee-flavoured fondant icings and filled with a sweet chantilly cream, are as dainty as can be.

50 g/3½ tablespoons butter, chilled and cubed
65 g/½ cup plain/all-purpose flour, sifted twice
2 eggs, beaten

for the chantilly cream
300 ml/1¼ cups double/heavy cream
seeds from 1 vanilla pod/bean
about 1–2 tablespoons icing/confectioners' sugar

to decorate
250 g/1¾ cups powdered fondant icing sugar
3 food flavourings and/or colourings of your choice

2 baking sheets, greased and lined with baking parchment
2 piping bags fitted with round nozzles/tips

makes 30

Preheat the oven to 200°C (400°F) Gas 6.

Heat the butter in a saucepan with 150 ml/⅔ cup cold water until the butter is melted. Bring to the boil, then quickly add the sifted flour all in one go and remove from the heat. Beat hard with a wooden spoon or whisk until the dough forms a ball and no longer sticks to the sides of the pan. Leave to cool for about 5 minutes. Whisk the eggs, then beat into the dough a small amount at a time using a balloon whisk. The mixture will form a sticky paste which holds its shape when you lift the whisk up.

Spoon the batter into a piping bag and pipe 30 small lines about 5 cm/2 inches long onto the baking sheet, a small distance apart. With clean hands, wet your finger and smooth down any peaks from the piping. Bake in the preheated oven for 10 minutes, then with a sharp knife cut a small slit into each éclair and return to the oven for a further 3–5 minutes, until crisp. Leave to cool on a wire rack, then cut each in half.

To make the chantilly cream, whip the cream with the vanilla seeds until the cream reaches stiff peaks. Sift in the icing/confectioners' sugar and fold through gently. Spoon the cream into the remaining piping bag and pipe into the éclairs.

To make the icings, mix the fondant icing sugar with 2 tablespoons water and divide into three bowls, colouring each with a very small amount of food colourings and/or flavourings of your choice. Spread the icing onto the éclairs using a round-bladed knife and leave to set before serving.

Serve immediately or store in the refrigerator until needed.

blackcurrant millefeuilles

a 375-g/13-oz. package all-butter
    puff pastry (thawed if frozen)
1 egg, beaten
caster/superfine sugar,
    for sprinkling
icing/confectioners' sugar,
    for dusting

for the filling
200 ml/¾ cup double/heavy
    cream
2 generous tablespoons
    blackcurrant preserve

*a baking sheet, greased and lined
    with baking parchment*
*a piping bag fitted with a small
    star nozzle/tip*

makes 24

*Millefeuilles — or thousand leaves — is a delicious French pastry
that is also known as the Napoleon. In a twist on the traditional
filling of vanilla custard, these pastries contain blackcurrant
preserve — a sharp fruity burst, perfectly offsetting the cream
and sugar dusting.*

Preheat the oven to 180°C (350°F)
Gas 4.

On a flour dusted surface, roll out
the pastry to a rectangle about 3 mm/
⅛ inch thick. Cut into 6 strips of
30 x 4 cm/12 x 2 inches and transfer
to the prepared baking sheet using
a large spatula, leaving a gap between
each strip of pastry. Brush with the
beaten egg and sprinkle over a little
caster/superfine sugar.

Bake the pastry in the preheated oven
for 12–15 minutes, until risen and golden
brown on top. Transfer to a wire rack
and leave to cool completely.

When you are ready to assemble the
millefeuilles, cut each pastry strip into
8 small squares.

Whip the cream to stiff peaks and
spoon into the piping bag. Pipe a row of
small cream stars onto half of the pastry
squares, top with a small spoonful of
blackcurrant preserve, then cover with
a second pastry square. Repeat until
all the pastry squares are filled, then
dust the tops of each pastry with icing/
confectioners' sugar.

Serve immediately or store in the
refrigerator until needed.

caramel paris brest

50 g/3½ tablespoons butter, chilled and cubed

65 g/½ cup plain/all-purpose flour, sifted twice

2 eggs, beaten

caramel curls, to decorate

for the cream liqueur filling

300 ml/1¼ cups double/heavy cream

1 tablespoon Bailey's or other whiskey cream liqueur

for the caramel fondant icing

200g/1⅔ cups powdered fondant icing sugar

2 tablespoons caramel sauce

2 baking sheets, greased and lined with baking parchment

2 piping bags fitted with round nozzles/tips

makes 18

Paris brest — the classic French choux rings — are traditionally made with coffee, but this delicious version features a caramel icing and a rich whiskey cream liqueur filling.

Preheat the oven to 200°C (400°F) Gas 6.

Heat the butter in a saucepan with 150 ml/⅔ cup cold water until the butter is melted. Bring to the boil, then quickly add the sifted flour all in one go and remove from the heat. Beat hard with a wooden spoon or whisk until the dough forms a ball and no longer sticks to the sides of the pan. Leave to cool for about 5 minutes. Whisk the eggs, then beat into the dough a small amount at a time using a balloon whisk. The mixture will form a sticky paste which holds its shape when you lift the whisk up.

Spoon the choux pastry dough into one of the piping bags and pipe 18 rings of 6 cm/2½ inches diameter a small distance apart. With clean hands wet your finger and smooth down any peaks from the piping so that the rings are

round. Bake in the preheated oven for 10 minutes, then with a sharp knife cut a small slit into each ring and return to the oven for 3–5 minutes until crisp. Leave to cool on a wire rack and then slice each in half horizontally.

To make the cream filling, add the liqueur to the cream and whip to stiff peaks using a whisk. Spoon into the second piping bag and pipe balls of cream between the choux ring halves.

To make the caramel fondant icing, mix 2 tablespoons cold water with the fondant icing sugar and the caramel sauce until you have a smooth thick icing. Using a round-bladed knife, spread the icing over the tops of the rings and decorate with caramel curls.

Serve immediately or store in the refrigerator until needed.

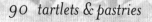

rose petal religieuses

50 g/3½ tablespoons butter, chilled and cubed
65 g/½ cup plain/all-purpose flour, sifted twice
2 eggs, beaten
silver dragées, to decorate

for the rose cream
2 tablespoons rose syrup
500 ml/2 cups double/heavy cream

for the fondant icing
1 tablespoon rose syrup
200 g/1⅔ cups powdered fondant icing sugar
pink food colouring

2 baking sheets, greased and lined with baking parchment
2 piping bags fitted with small round nozzles/tips and 1 piping bag fitted with a very small star nozzle/tip

makes 18

Religieuse is the French word for nun and these cute choux buns are said to resemble nuns in their habits. Be as adventurous as you like with the decoration — the traditional finish is cream piped in vertical lines and a silver dragée, but rosettes of cream look equally pretty.

Preheat the oven to 200°C (400°F) Gas 6.

Heat the butter in a saucepan with 150 ml/⅔ cup cold water until the butter is melted. Bring to the boil, then quickly add the sifted flour all in one go and remove from the heat. Beat hard with a wooden spoon or whisk until the dough forms a ball and no longer sticks to the sides of the pan. Leave to cool for about 5 minutes. Whisk the eggs, then beat into the dough a small amount at a time using a balloon whisk. The mixture will form a sticky paste which holds its shape when you lift the whisk up.

Spoon the choux pastry dough into one of the piping bags fitted with a round nozzle and pipe 18 rings of 5 cm/2 inches diameter and 18 small balls 1 cm/½ inch diameter. With clean hands, wet your finger and smooth down any peaks from the piping so that the rings and balls are round. Bake the pastry in the preheated oven for 10 minutes, then with a sharp knife cut a small slit into each ring and ball and return to the oven for a further 3–5 minutes, until crisp. Leave to cool on a wire rack, then cut each in half.

To make the rose cream, add the rose syrup to the cream and whip to stiff peaks using a whisk. Spoon into the second piping bag fitted with a round nozzle/tip and pipe between the choux ring halves and fill the balls. Reserve some of the cream for decoration.

To make the fondant icing, mix together the rose syrup, powdered fondant icing sugar, 1 tablespoon cold water and a drop of food colouring to achieve a pale pink. Using a round-bladed knife, spread the icing over the tops of the rings. Place a choux ball on top of each ring and ice the top of the balls. Put the reserved rose cream in the piping bag fitted with a very small star nozzle/tip and pipe decorations on the buns, as desired. Top with a silver dragée.

Serve immediately or store in the refrigerator until needed.

chocolate profiteroles

50 g/3½ tablespoons butter, chilled and cubed

65 g/½ cup plain/all-purpose flour, sifted twice

2 eggs, beaten

300 ml/1¼ cups double/heavy cream

for the chocolate sauce

80 g/2½ oz. dark/bittersweet chocolate (70% cocoa solids)

30 g/2 tablespoons butter

2 tablespoons double/heavy cream

2 tablespoons golden syrup/light corn syrup

2 baking sheets, greased and lined with baking parchment

2 piping bags fitted with round nozzles/tips

seves 8

These are classic Italian profiteroles, just a little bit tinier. Minute dots of choux pastry, filled with whipped cream and drizzled with a rich chocolate sauce, are piled high in a dessertspoon in individual portions.

Preheat the oven to 200°C (400°F) Gas 6.

Heat the butter in a saucepan with 150 ml/⅔ cup cold water until the butter is melted. Bring to the boil, then quickly add the sifted flour all in one go and remove from the heat. Beat hard with a wooden spoon or whisk until the dough forms a ball and no longer sticks to the sides of the pan. Leave to cool for about 5 minutes. Whisk the eggs, then beat into the dough a small amount at a time using a balloon whisk. The mixture will form a sticky paste which holds its shape when you lift the whisk up.

Spoon the choux pastry dough into one of the piping bags and pipe 80 small 1-cm/½-inch balls onto the prepared baking sheets, a small distance apart. With clean hands, wet your finger and smooth down any peaks from the piping so that the balls are round. Bake in the preheated oven for 10 minutes, then with a sharp knife cut a small slit into each ball and return to the oven for 3–5 minutes, until crisp. Leave to cool on a wire rack, then carefully cut each one in half.

Whip the cream to stiff peaks, spoon it into the second piping bag and fill each profiterole with it.

To make the chocolate sauce, heat the chocolate, butter, cream and syrup in a saucepan until the chocolate has melted and the sauce is smooth and glossy.

To serve, arrange small piles of filled profiteroles in dessertspoons, drizzle with the warm chocolate sauce and serve immediately.

summer berry tartlets

110 g/¾ cup plain/all-purpose
   flour, plus extra for dusting
60 g/½ stick butter
30 g/2 tablespoons caster/
   superfine sugar
1 egg yolk
a few drops of vanilla extract

for the crème pâtissière
1 tablespoon cornflour/
   cornstarch
60 g/⅓ cup caster/granulated
   sugar
1 egg and 1 egg yolk
100 ml/scant ½ cup milk
150 ml/⅔ cup double/heavy
   cream
1 vanilla pod/bean, split
   lengthways

to assemble
200 g/1½ cups summer berries
3 tablespoons apricot preserve
freshly squeezed juice of 2 small
   lemons

*a round fluted cutter (6 cm/2½
   inches diameter)*
24 mini tartlet pans, greased
baking beans
*a piping bag fitted with a round
   nozzle/tip*

makes 24

These crisp pastry tartlets, filled with classic crème pâtissière and topped with glazed summer berries, are guaranteed to disappear very quickly whenever you serve them!

To make the pastry, sift the flour into a mixing bowl and rub in the butter until the mixture resembles fine breadcrumbs. Add the sugar, egg yolk and vanilla extract and mix together to a soft dough with your fingers, adding a little cold water if the mixture is too dry. Wrap in clingfilm/plastic wrap and chill in the refrigerator for 1 hour.

Preheat the oven to 180°C (350°F) Gas 4.

On a flour dusted surface, roll out the pastry to a thickness of 3 mm/⅜ inch. Stamp out 24 rounds using the cutter and press one into each hole in the pan, trimming away any excess pastry. Chill in the refrigerator for 30 minutes. Line each pastry case with baking parchment and fill with baking beans. Bake in the preheated oven for 12–15 minutes, until golden brown and crisp. Leave to cool in the pans for 10 minutes, then transfer to a wire rack and leave to cool completely.

To prepare the crème pâtissière, whisk together the cornflour/cornstarch, sugar, egg and egg yolk until creamy. Put the milk, cream and split vanilla pod/bean in a saucepan and bring to the boil. Pour over the egg mixture, whisking all the time. Return to the pan and cook for a few minutes until thick, then remove the vanilla pod/bean. Pass the mixture through a sieve/strainer to remove any lumps and set aside to cool.

To assemble, spoon the crème pâtissière into the piping bag and pipe it into the pastry cases. Top each one with berries.

Put the apricot preserve and lemon juice in a small saucepan and heat until blended. Pass through a sieve/strainer to remove any bits and, using a pastry brush, brush the mixture over each tartlet to glaze.

These tartlets are best eaten on the day they are made.

little maids of honour

110 g/¾ cup plus 2 tablespoons plain/all-purpose flour, plus extra for dusting
60 g/½ stick butter
30 g/2½ tablespoons caster/granulated sugar
1 egg yolk

for the filling
3 tablespoons lemon curd or other fruit preserve
3 tablespoons mascarpone
50 g/⅓ cup whole blanched almonds
50 g/1½ oz. sliced brioche or challah bread
60 g/½ stick butter, softened
2 tablespoons caster/superfine sugar
1 large egg
1 teaspoon vanilla extract
finely grated zest of 1 lemon

to decorate
24 whole blanched almond halves (ideally Marcona)
icing/confectioner's sugar, for dusting

a 24-hole mini muffin pan, greased
a flower-shaped cutter (6 cm/2½ inches diameter)
a piping bag fitted with a large round nozzle/tip

makes 24

These traditional English tartlets filled with almond paste and fruit preserve, have their origins in Tudor times and are said to have been a favourite of Anne Boleyn's. Similar to Bakewell tarts, they make an elegant gift for any hostess.

To make the pastry, sift the flour into a mixing bowl and rub in the butter until the mixture resembles fine breadcrumbs. Add the sugar and egg yolk and mix together to a soft dough with your fingertips, adding a little cold water if the mixture is too dry. Wrap the dough in clingfilm/plastic wrap and chill in the refrigerator for 1 hour.

Preheat the oven 180°C (350°F) Gas 4.

On a flour dusted surface, roll out the pastry to a thickness of 3 mm/⅛ inch. Stamp out 24 flower shapes with the cutter and put one in each hole of the muffin pan, pressing them tightly against the base and side of the pan. Chill in the refrigerator until needed.

Spoon about ⅓ teaspoon each of lemon curd and mascarpone into the bottom of each pastry case.

Put the almonds and brioche in a food processor and blitz to a fine crumb.

Cream together the butter and sugar, then add the egg, vanilla extract, lemon zest and almond and brioche mixture. Mix everything well, then spoon into the piping bag. Pipe a small amount of filling into each tartlet case to fill. Top each one with an almond half and bake in the preheated oven for 12–15 minutes, until golden brown.

Dust each tart with icing/confectioners' sugar and serve warm or cold.

chocolate & salted caramel tartlets

80 g/⅔ cup plain/all-purpose
    flour, plus extra for dusting
2 tablespoons cocoa powder
60 g/½ stick butter
2 tablespoons caster/
    granulated sugar
1 egg yolk
12 silver dragées, to decorate

for the salted caramel
100 g/½ cup caster/granulated
    sugar
60 g/½ stick butter
½ teaspoon salt
1 tablespoon double/heavy
    cream

for the chocolate ganache
100 g/3½ oz. dark/bittersweet
    chocolate
60 ml/¼ cup double/heavy cream
30 g/2 tablespoons butter
1 tablespoon golden syrup/light
    corn syrup

*12 mini tartlet pans (6 cm/2½ inches
    square), greased*
baking beans

makes 12

The combination of fashionable salted caramel and rich chocolate ganache makes these a sophisticated treat that's guaranteed to delight chocoholics everywhere.

To make the pastry, sift the flour and cocoa powder into a mixing bowl and rub in the butter until the mixture resembles fine breadcrumbs. Add the sugar and egg yolk and mix together to a soft dough with your fingers, adding a little cold water if the mixture is too dry. Wrap the dough in clingfilm/plastic wrap and chill in the refrigerator for 1 hour.

Preheat the oven to 180°C (350°F) Gas 4.

On a flour dusted surface, roll out the pastry to a thickness of 3 mm/⅛ inch. Use a sharp knife to cut out 12 squares slightly larger than the baking pans and press one into each pan, trimming away any excess pastry. Chill in the refrigerator for 30 minutes. Line each tartlet case with baking parchment and fill with baking beans. Bake in the preheated oven for 12–15 minutes, until crisp. Transfer to a wire rack and leave to cool completely.

To make the salted caramel, heat the sugar with 2 tablespoons water in a saucepan set over gentle heat. Remove the pan from the heat as soon the mixture starts to turn golden brown. Add the butter, salt and cream and return to the heat, stirring, until the butter has melted. Pour a little of the mixture into the base of each cooled tartlet case.

To make the chocolate ganache, put the chocolate, cream and butter in a heatproof bowl set over a pan of barely simmering water. (Take care that the base of the bowl does not touch the water.) Stir until the chocolate and butter have melted and blended. Remove the pan from the heat and beat in the syrup.

Pour a little of the ganache into each tartlet case. Leave to partially set then top with a silver dragée. Leave to set completely before serving.

individual plum tartes tatin

Caramelized tartes tatin, with their rich buttery pastry and dark sugary caramel, are quite simply delicious. Whilst normally served as a large tart, these individual ones make the perfect sweet treat. You can substitute other fruits, such as apple, pear or pineapple, if you prefer.

100 g/½ cup caster/granulated
   sugar
50 g/3½ tablespoons butter
6 ripe plums
60 g/2 oz. golden marzipan
plain/all-purpose flour,
   for dusting
a 375-g/13-oz. package all-butter
   puff pastry (thawed if frozen)
custard or whipped cream,
   to serve

a 12-hole muffin pan, greased
a round cutter (9 cm/3½ inches
   diameter)

makes 12

Preheat the oven to 180°C (350°F) Gas 4.

Put the sugar and butter in a small saucepan and warm over gentle heat, until the sugar dissolves and then allow it to caramelize and turn golden brown, taking care that it does not burn. Remove from the heat immediately and put a spoonful of caramel into each hole of the pan.

Cut the plums in half, and remove the stones/pits. Place one plum half, cut-side up, in each hole of the pan.

Break the marzipan into 12 pieces of equal size and roll them into balls.

Place one ball into each plum, where the stone/pit once was.

On a flour dusted surface, roll the pastry out to a thickness of 3 mm/⅜ inch. Stamp out 12 rounds with the cutter. Cover each plum with a pastry round, pressing the pastry tightly into the holes.

Bake the tarts in the preheated oven for 12–15 minutes, until the pastry is crisp and the plums are soft. Remove from the oven, leave to cool for a few minutes, then remove each tatin with a spoon and invert.

Serve the tatins warm or cold with cream or custard.

caramelized tartes au citron

These melt-in-the-mouth tartlets are mini versions of a classic French lemon tart — a delicious combination of buttery pastry, tangy lemon cream filling and a caramelized sugar topping.

110 g/¾ cup plain/all-purpose
  flour, plus extra for dusting
60 g/½ stick butter
finely grated zest of 2 lemons
2 tablespoons caster/superfine
  sugar
1 egg yolk
icing/confectioners' sugar,
  for dusting

for the lemon filling
100 ml/⅓ cup double/heavy
  cream
finely grated zest and juice
  of 1 lemon
50 g/¼ cup caster/granulated
  sugar
1 egg

20 oval mini tartlet pans
  (8 cm/3¼ inches long), greased
baking beans
a chef's blow torch (optional)

makes 20

To make the pastry, sift the flour into a mixing bowl and rub in the butter until the mixture resembles fine breadcrumbs. Add the lemon zest, sugar and egg yolk and mix together to a soft dough with your fingertips, adding a little cold water if the mixture is too dry. Wrap the dough in clingfilm/plastic wrap and chill in the refrigerator for 1 hour.

Preheat the oven to 180°C (350°F) Gas 4.

On a flour dusted surface, roll out the pastry to a thickness of 3 mm/⅛ inch. Use a sharp knife to cut out 20 oval pieces of pastry and press one into each tartlet pan, trimming the edges

with a sharp knife. Put a piece of baking parchment in each pastry case, fill with baking beans and bake in the preheated oven for 10–15 minutes, until the pastry is crisp. Do not turn off the oven.

To make the lemon filling, whisk together the cream, lemon juice and zest, sugar and egg and pour into each pastry case. Bake the tartlets in the preheated oven for 10–15 minutes, until the filling has set.

Dust the tarts liberally with sifted icing/confectioners' sugar, then caramelize the sugar using a chef's blow torch or under a hot grill/broiler. Leave to cool before serving.

mini lemon & lime meringue pies

These little pies are full of tangy citrus curd, topped with a fluffy meringue and encased in crisp chocolate shortcake.

60 g/½ cup plain/all-purpose flour, plus extra for dusting
1 tablespoon cocoa powder
60 g/½ stick butter, chilled
25 g/2 tablespoons caster/granulated sugar

for the citrus curd
80 ml/⅓ cup lemon and lime juice (roughly 2 lemons and 3 limes)
60 g/½ stick butter
115 g/⅓ cup plus 1 tablespoon caster/granulated sugar
2 eggs, beaten

for the meringue
100 g/½ cup caster/superfine sugar
40 ml/2½ tablespoons golden syrup/light corn syrup
2 large egg whites

24 fluted tartlet pans (5 cm/2 inch diameter), greased
baking beans
a piping bag fitted with a large star nozzle/tip
a chef's blow torch (optional)

makes 24

To make the citrus curd, put the juice, butter and sugar in a heatproof bowl set over a pan of simmering water and whisk until the sugar has dissolved. Add the beaten eggs, whisking continuously, until the mixture thickens. Pass through a sieve/strainer to remove any lumps. Leave to cool, then store in the refrigerator until needed.

To make the pastry, sift the flour and cocoa powder into a mixing bowl and rub in the butter with your fingertips, until the mixture resembles fine breadcrumbs. Add the sugar, and a little cold water if the mixture is too dry, and work the pastry with your hands until it comes together into a ball. Wrap in clingfilm/plastic wrap and chill in the refrigerator for 1 hour.

Preheat the oven to 180°C (350°F) Gas 4.

On a flour dusted surface, roll out the pastry to a thickness of about 3 mm/⅛ inch. Cut out rounds of pastry slightly larger than the tart pans with a sharp knife. Press a round of pastry into each pan, trimming away any excess with a sharp knife. Transfer to the refrigerator for 30 minutes, then remove, line each pan with baking parchment and fill with baking beans. Bake in the preheated oven for 10–15 minutes, until the tarts cases are crisp. Turn out onto a wire rack and leave to cool. Fill each case with the citrus curd.

To make the meringue, heat the sugar, syrup and 2½ tablespoons water in a saucepan, until the sugar has dissolved and bring to the boil. Put the egg whites in a bowl and whisk to a stiff peak. Pour in the hot sugar syrup and whisk continuously until the meringue is cold. Spoon the meringue into the piping bag and pipe a swirl on top of the curd.

Lightly brown the meringue with a chef's blow torch or under a grill/broiler.

Serve the pies immediately or store in the refrigerator until needed.

macarons & meringues

Stylish, picture-perfect and delicious, French macarons are the ultimate in pretty sweet treats. Hold a single apricot & almond macaron between your fingers and before you've even bitten through the crisp then chewy shell, and into the vibrant filling, you are transported to a table outside a Parisian salon de thé. Deliciously simple meringues are as endlessly adaptable as macarons — whether they are romantic meringue kisses piled up on an elegant cake stand and garnished with rose petals for a wedding display, or colourful super-duper disco meringues served at a child's birthday party. Whichever you choose, both macarons and meringues make a perfect gift or talking point at an elegant afternoon tea.

salted caramel macarons

for the basic macarons

**200 g/½ cups icing/confectioners'
sugar**

100 g/⅔ cup ground almonds

**120–125 g/½ cup egg whites
(about 3 eggs)**

a pinch of salt

**40 g/3 tablespoons caster/
superfine sugar**

for the salted caramel filling

**75 g/⅓ cup caster/superfine
sugar**

**75 g/1⅓ cup light muscovado/
light brown sugar**

**50 g/3 tablespoons unsalted
butter**

**100 ml/½ cup double/heavy
cream**

½ teaspoon sea salt flakes

*a piping bag fitted with a 1-cm/
½-inch round nozzle/tip*

*2 heavy baking sheets, lined with
baking parchment*

makes 20

*Salted caramel seems to be the flavour of the moment, and the
combination works like a dream sandwiched in macarons.*

To make the basic macarons, tip the
icing/confectioners' sugar and almonds
into the bowl of a food processor and
blend for 30 seconds until thoroughly
combined. Set aside.

Tip the egg whites into a spotlessly
clean and dry mixing bowl. Add the salt
and, using an electric hand whisk, beat
until they will only just hold a stiff peak.
Continue to whisk at medium speed
while adding the caster/superfine sugar a
teaspoonful at a time. Mix well between
each addition to ensure the sugar is
thoroughly incorporated before adding
the next spoonful. The mixture should
be thick, white and glossy.

Using a large metal spoon, fold the
ground sugar and almond mixture into
the egg whites. The mixture should be
thoroughly incorporated and smooth –
this can take up to 1 minute. When it
is ready, the mixture drops from the
spoon in a smooth molten mass.

Pipe rounds of mixture onto the
prepared baking sheets. Tap the baking
sheets sharply on the work surface to
expel any large air bubbles. Leave the
macarons to rest for 15 minutes–1 hour,
until they have 'set' and formed a dry

shell. They should not be sticky, tacky
or wet when tested with your fingertip.

Preheat the oven to 170°C (325°F)
Gas 3.

Bake the macarons on the middle shelf
of the preheated oven, one sheet at a
time, for 10 minutes. The tops should
be crisp and the bottoms dry. Leave to
cool on the baking sheet.

To make the salted caramel filling,
put the caster/superfine sugar and
2 tablespoons water in a small saucepan
over low heat and let the sugar dissolve
completely. Bring to the boil, then
cook until the syrup turns to an amber-
coloured caramel. Remove from the
heat and add the muscovado/brown
sugar, butter and cream. Stir to dissolve,
then return to the low heat and simmer
for 3–4 minutes, until the caramel has
thickened and will coat the back of a
spoon. Remove from the heat, add the
salt, pour into a bowl and leave until
completely cold and thick.

Spread the filling over half the macaron
shells and sandwich with the other half.
Leave to rest for about 30 minutes
before serving.

rose macarons

1 quantity Basic Macarons recipe
    (see page 110)
pink food colouring paste
½ teaspoon rose water
1 tablespoon rose sprinkles or
    crystallized rose petals, finely
    chopped

for the rose buttercream
125 g/1 stick unsalted butter,
    softened
250 g/1⅔ cups icing/
    confectioners' sugar, sifted
½ teaspoon rosewater

a piping bag fitted with a 1-cm/
*   ½-inch round nozzle/tip*
2 heavy baking sheets, lined with
*   baking parchment*
a piping bag fitted with a star
*   nozzle/tip*

makes 20

*You could make boxes of these dainty rose-infused macarons
in varying shades of pink — perfect for a fancy afternoon tea
with the girls.*

Prepare the Basic Macarons according to the recipe on page 110, adding the pink food colouring paste and rose water to the meringue mixture before you fold in the ground sugar and almonds. (Add the food colouring paste slowly, dipping a cocktail stick into the paste and then into the mixture, mixing well to ensure that the colour is evenly blended.)

Use the piping bag with the round nozzle/tip to pipe rounds of mixture onto the prepared baking sheets. Tap the baking sheets sharply on the work surface to expel any large air bubbles, then scatter rose sprinkles or petals over the tops. Leave the macarons to rest for 15 minutes–1 hour.

Preheat the oven to 170°C (325°F) Gas 3.

Bake the macarons on the middle shelf of the preheated oven, one sheet at a time, for 10 minutes. Leave to cool on the baking sheet.

To make the rose buttercream, beat the butter until creamy and pale. Gradually add the sifted icing/confectioners' sugar, beating well until the buttercream is smooth, then add the rosewater and mix well to combine.

Fill the piping bag fitted with the star nozzle/tip with the buttercream and pipe it onto half the macaron shells. Sandwich with the other half and leave to rest for about 30 minutes before serving.

apricot & almond macarons

1 quantity Basic Macarons recipe
   (see page 110)
yellow food colouring paste
red and yellow liquid food
   colouring

for the apricot filling
150 g/1 cup ready-to-eat dried
   apricots
1 tablespoon lemon juice
1 tablespoon honey
2–3 tablespoons Amaretto or
   apricot brandy
4 generous tablespoons
   mascarpone

a piping bag fitted with a 1-cm/
   ½-inch round nozzle/tip
2 heavy baking sheets, lined with
   baking parchment
a clean toothbrush

makes 20

Decorate the top of these macarons with speckles of yellow and red liquid food colouring. When they're in season you could also purée fresh apricots for the filling.

Start making the filling the day before making the macaron shells.

Roughly chop the apricots and put them in a saucepan with the lemon juice, honey and Amaretto or apricot brandy. Heat gently but do not boil. Remove from the heat and leave the apricots to soak overnight until plump and juicy.

The next day, whiz the apricots and any remaining soaking liquid in a food processor until they are as smooth as possible. Add the mascarpone and pulse just until incorporated. Spoon the filling into a bowl, cover and chill in the refrigerator until needed.

Prepare the Basic Macarons according to the recipe on page 110, adding the yellow food colouring paste to the meringue mixture before you fold in the ground sugar and almonds. (Add the food colouring paste slowly, dipping a cocktail stick into the paste and then into the mixture, mixing well to ensure that the colour is evenly blended.)

Pipe rounds of mixture onto the prepared baking sheets. Tap the baking sheets sharply on the work surface to expel any large air bubbles. Trickle a little red food colouring onto a saucer, then dip the clean toothbrush into it. Flick the bristles over the macarons so that they are flecked with red. Repeat with the yellow colouring. Leave the macarons to rest for 15 minutes–1 hour.

Preheat the oven to 170°C (325°F) Gas 3.

Bake the macarons on the middle shelf of the preheated oven, one sheet at a time, for 10 minutes. Leave to cool on the baking sheet.

Spread the filling over half the macaron shells and sandwich with the other half. Leave to rest for about 30 minutes before serving.

blueberry & vanilla macarons

1 quantity Basic Macarons recipe
    (page 110)
purple food colouring paste
pink or purple sugar sprinkles

for the blueberry filling
300 g/3 cups blueberries
1 tablespoon granulated sugar

for the vanilla cream
3 egg yolks
75 g/¾ cup caster/superfine
    sugar
1 tablespoon cornflour/
    cornstarch
250 ml/1 cup full-fat milk
1 vanilla pod/bean, split
    lengthways
3 tablespoons unsalted butter,
    cubed
100 ml/½ cup double/heavy
    cream

*2 heavy baking sheets, lined with
    baking parchment*
*a piping bag fitted with a star
    nozzle/tip*

makes 20

*Try piping these macarons into delicate fingers instead of
the usual round shapes and fill with blueberry purée, fresh
blueberries and a delicate vanilla cream.*

Prepare the Basic Macarons according to the recipe on page 110, adding the purple food colouring paste to the meringue mixture before you fold in the ground sugar and almonds. (Add the food colouring paste slowly, dipping a cocktail stick into the paste and then into the mixture, mixing well to ensure that the colour is evenly blended.)

Pipe 6-cm/2½-inch-long fingers of mixture onto the prepared baking sheets. Tap the baking sheets sharply on the work surface to expel any large air bubbles, then scatter sugar sprinkles over the tops. Leave the macarons to rest for 15 minutes–1 hour.

Preheat the oven to 170°C (325°F) Gas 3.

Bake the macarons on the middle shelf of the preheated oven, one sheet at a time, for 10 minutes. Leave to cool on the baking sheet.

For the blueberry filling, tip half of the blueberries into a small saucepan, add the sugar and 1 tablespoon water and cook over medium heat until the berries soften and burst, then continue to cook until thickened to a jam-like consistency. Transfer the berries to a nylon sieve/

strainer and press through with the back of a spoon into a bowl, discarding the sieve/strainer contents. Set aside to cool.

To make the vanilla cream, put the egg yolks, sugar and cornflour/cornstarch in a small, heatproof bowl and whisk together until combined.

Heat the milk, along with the vanilla pod/bean, in a small saucepan until it only just starts to boil. Remove the vanilla and pour the hot milk over the egg mixture, whisking constantly until smooth. Pour the mixture back into the pan and cook gently over low heat, stirring constantly until the custard comes to the boil and thickens. Strain into a clean bowl, add the butter and stir until the butter has melted and is incorporated into the mixture. Cover the surface with clingfilm/plastic wrap and leave to cool before refrigerating.

Whip the cream until it will hold soft peaks and fold into the chilled custard.

Spread the blueberry filling over half the macaron shells and arrange the whole blueberries on top, spaced apart. Pipe the vanilla cream between the blueberries and top with the remaining macaron shells.

cappuccino macarons

Pipe the filling into these delicate coffee-flavoured macarons in an extra-thick layer.

1 quantity Basic Macarons recipe (page 110)
2 teaspoons coffee extract or 2 teaspoons instant coffee granules dissolved in 1 teaspoon boiling water
brown food colouring paste
cocoa powder, for dusting

for the coffee cream filling
3 egg yolks
75 g/³⁄₄ cup caster/superfine sugar
1 tablespoon cornflour/cornstarch
250 ml/1 cup full-fat milk
1 vanilla pod/bean, split lengthways
3 tablespoons unsalted butter, cubed
100 ml/¹⁄₂ cup double/heavy cream
1 teaspoon coffee extract

2 piping bags fitted with 1-cm/¹⁄₂-inch round nozzles/tips
2 heavy baking sheets, lined with baking parchment

makes 20

Prepare the Basic Macarons according to the recipe on page 110, adding the brown food colouring paste and coffee extract to the meringue mixture before you fold in the ground sugar and almonds. (Add the food colouring paste slowly, dipping a cocktail stick into the paste and then into the mixture, mixing well to ensure that the colour is evenly blended.)

Pipe rounds of mixture onto the prepared baking sheets. Tap the baking sheets sharply on the work surface to expel any large air bubbles, then lightly dust cocoa powder over the tops. Leave the macarons to rest for 15 minutes–1 hour.

Preheat the oven to 170°C (325°F) Gas 3.

Bake the macarons on the middle shelf of the preheated oven, one sheet at a time, for 10 minutes. Leave to cool on the baking sheet.

To make the coffee cream filling, put the egg yolks, sugar and cornflour/cornstarch in a small, heatproof bowl and whisk together until combined.

Heat the milk, along with the vanilla pod/bean, in a small saucepan until it only just starts to boil. Remove the vanilla and pour the hot milk over the egg mixture, whisking constantly until smooth. Pour the mixture back into the pan and cook gently over low heat, stirring constantly until the custard comes to the boil and thickens. Strain into a clean bowl, add the butter and stir until the butter has melted and is incorporated into the mixture. Cover the surface with clingfilm/plastic wrap and leave to cool before refrigerating.

Whip the cream until it will hold soft peaks and fold into the chilled custard along with the coffee extract.

Fill the other piping bag with the coffee cream and pipe it onto half the macaron shells. Pipe two or three layers of filling to make an extra-generous filling. Sandwich with the other half of the shells and leave to rest for about 30 minutes before serving.

chocolate & passion fruit macarons

1 quantity **Basic Macarons recipe**
(see page 110)
yellow food colouring paste
chocolate sprinkles or flakes

for the chocolate passion fruit filling
6 passion fruit
150 g/5 oz. dark/bittersweet
chocolate, finely chopped
150 ml/²⁄₃ cup double/heavy
cream
1 tablespoon light muscovado/
light brown sugar
a pinch of salt

a piping bag fitted with a 1-cm/
½-inch round nozzle/tip
2 heavy baking sheets, lined with baking parchment

makes 20

First you taste the chocolate, and then the passion-fruit flavour hits you in an unexpected and delicious way.

Prepare the Basic Macarons according to the recipe on page 110, adding the yellow food colouring paste to the meringue mixture before you fold in the ground sugar and almonds. (Add the food colouring paste slowly, dipping a cocktail stick into the paste and then into the mixture, mixing well to ensure that the colour is evenly blended.)

Pipe rounds of mixture onto the prepared baking sheets. Tap the baking sheets sharply on the work surface to expel any large air bubbles, then scatter the chocolate sprinkles over the tops. Leave the macarons to rest for 15 minutes–1 hour.

Preheat the oven to 170°C (325°F) Gas 3.

Bake the macarons on the middle shelf of the preheated oven, one sheet at a time, for 10 minutes. Leave to cool on the baking sheet.

To make the filling, cut the passion fruit in half and scoop the seeds and juice into a nylon sieve/strainer set over a small saucepan. Using the back of spoon, press the pulp through the sieve/strainer – you should end up with about 4–5 tablespoons of juice. Set the pan over low–medium heat and bring slowly to the boil. Cook gently until the juice has reduced by half and you have about 1–2 tablespoons thick passion-fruit juice remaining.

Put the chocolate in a small, heatproof bowl. Put the cream and sugar in a small saucepan and heat until the sugar has dissolved and the cream has come to the boil. Add the salt, then pour the hot cream over the chopped chocolate and leave to melt. Stir until smooth and leave to set and thicken slightly before using.

Stir the thick passion-fruit juice into the chocolate ganache, then spread over half the macaron shells. Sandwich with the remaining macaron shells and leave to rest for 30 minutes before serving.

apple & blackberry macarons

1 quantity Basic Macarons recipe
(see page 110)
purple food colouring paste
green food colouring paste

for the apple and blackberry filling
4 small dessert apples,
such as Cox's or Winesap
1 tablespoon granulated sugar
freshly squeezed juice of
½ lemon
125 g/1 cup blackberries
100 ml/½ cup double/heavy
cream

*2 piping bags fitted with 1-cm/
½-inch round nozzles/tips*
*2 heavy baking sheets, lined with
baking parchment*
*a piping bag fitted with a star
nozzle/tip*

makes 20

Here's a classic autumnal fruit combination that works perfectly in macarons not only because it tastes great, but also because the colours complement each other.

Prepare the filling before you make the macaron shells.

Peel, core and roughly chop the apples and place in a saucepan with the sugar and lemon juice. Cover and cook over low heat until the fruit has started to soften, stirring from time to time. Add the blackberries and continue to cook for a further 10–15 minutes until the fruit has reduced to a thick purée. Remove from the heat and press through a nylon sieve/strainer into a small bowl. Taste and add a little more sugar, if needed.

Begin to prepare the Basic Macarons according to the recipe on page 110. Once all the sugar is incorporated into the egg whites, divide the mixture between 2 bowls and add purple food colouring paste to one bowl and green food colouring paste to the other. (Add the food colouring paste slowly, dipping a cocktail stick into the paste and then into the mixture, mixing well to ensure that the colour is evenly blended.)

Continue with the basic recipe, dividing the ground almond and sugar mixture equally between the two bowls.

Use the piping bags fitted with the round nozzles/tips to pipe 20 rounds of each colour of mixture onto each prepared baking sheet. Tap the baking sheets sharply on the work surface to expel any large air bubbles, then leave the macarons to rest for 15 minutes–1 hour.

Preheat the oven to 170°C (325°F) Gas 3.

Bake the macarons on the middle shelf of the preheated oven, one sheet at a time, for 10 minutes. Leave to cool on the baking sheet.

Lightly whip the double/heavy cream. Spread the fruit filling onto the purple macaron shells. Fill the piping bag fitted with the star nozzle/tip with the whipped cream and pipe it onto the green shells. Sandwich the two together and leave to rest for about 30 minutes before serving.

meringue kisses

2 egg whites
**115 g/½ cup plus 1 tablespoon
caster/superfine sugar**

*a piping bag fitted with a large round
nozzle/tip*
*2 heavy baking sheets, lined with
baking parchment*

makes about 50

*There's something utterly irresistible about fluffy white
meringues. They look lovely piled up on cake stands and
scattered with pale pink rose petals. You could even serve them
with a little dish of clotted cream and fresh strawberries, too,
for guests to dunk.*

Preheat the oven to 110°C (225°F)
Gas ¼.

In a spotlessly clean, grease-free bowl,
whisk the egg whites with an electric
hand whisk until they stand in stiff peaks.
Gradually add the sugar, a spoonful at a
time, whisking between each addition
until the mixture is thick and glossy.

Spoon the meringue into the piping bag
and pipe swirls onto the prepared baking
sheets a small distance apart.

Transfer the meringues to the preheated
oven and bake for 1 hour until crisp and
dry. Remove from the oven and leave to
cool before serving.

chocolate & pistachio meringues

3 egg whites
a tiny pinch of salt
150 g/1¼ cups icing/confectioners'
    sugar, sifted
2 teaspoons cocoa powder, sifted
50 g/2 oz. dark/bittersweet
    chocolate, grated

for the pistachio cream
100 g/7 oz. white chocolate,
    broken up
50 ml/3 tablespoons double/
    heavy cream
50 g/½ cup shelled pistachios,
    finely ground
100 g/7 oz. dark/bittersweet
    chocolate
ground or shredded pistachios,
    to decorate

*2 heavy baking sheets, lined with
    baking parchment
a piping bag fitted with a plain or
    star nozzle/tip (optional)*

makes 30

These little meringues make a lovely display for a special tea or piled high instead of a birthday cake. Bright green shelled and shredded pistachios are available from Middle Eastern stores — buy them if you see them and store them in a container in the freezer and they will stay fresh for months.

Preheat the oven to 140°C (275°F) Gas 1.

To make the meringues, whisk the egg whites with the salt in a clean, grease-free bowl until quite firm. Gradually whisk in the icing/confectioners' sugar, a tablespoon at a time, making sure the meringue is as firm as possible between each addition of sugar. Mix the cocoa powder into the last tablespoon of sugar and whisk into the meringue, then quickly fold in the grated chocolate.

Either spoon tablespoons of the meringue onto the prepared baking sheets or fill the piping bag with the mixture and pipe in mounds or rosettes. Bake for 40 minutes, then switch off the oven and leave to cool in the oven. When cold, carefully lift the meringues off the paper.

To make the pistachio cream, put the white chocolate and cream in a small bowl and set over a pan of simmering water (making sure the bowl does not touch the water). Remove from the heat and leave to melt. Stir to combine, then leave to cool for five minutes. Stir in the ground pistachios, then leave to cool completely but don't refrigerate or the mixture will set too hard.

To assemble the meringues, melt the chocolate in a heatproof bowl set over a pan of simmering water. Dip the base of each meringue into the melted chocolate and leave on non-stick baking parchment to set. Sandwich pairs of meringues together with a little pistachio cream, then roll the meringue in the extra ground or shredded pistachios so that they stick to the cream.

super-duper disco meringues

300 g/1½ cups caster/superfine
    sugar
150 g/⅔ cup egg whites
    (about 4 large)
a pinch of salt

to decorate
2 food colouring pastes in
    colours of your choice
assorted coloured sugar
    sprinkles
600 ml/2½ cups double/heavy
    cream

a clean craft brush
3 large piping bags fitted with plain
    and/or star nozzles/tips
3 heavy baking sheets, lined with
    baking parchment

makes 30

*What child can resist a pile of colourful mini meringues?
These ones are sure to bring smiles to little faces at any birthday
party. Half of the meringues are decorated with coloured sugar
sprinkles and the other half marbled with red or blue food
colouring. No matter how many you make or in which colours,
these will disappear in a blink of an eye.*

Preheat the oven to 200°C (400°F)
Gas 6.

To make the meringue mixture, tip the
sugar into a small roasting pan and place
on the middle shelf of the preheated
oven for about 5 minutes or until hot to
the touch. When the sugar is ready, turn
the oven temperature down to 110°C
(225°F) Gas ¼.

Meanwhile, whisk the egg whites in the
bowl of a stand mixer until frothy. With
the motor running on low speed, tip the
hot sugar onto the egg whites in one go.
Turn the speed up to medium–high and
whisk for about 8 minutes or until the
meringue is very stiff, white and cold.
Divide the mixture between 3 bowls.

Using the clean craft brush, paint
3 fine, straight lines of one of the food
colouring pastes on the inside of a
piping bag, going from the nozzle/tip
towards the opening. Fill the bag with
one-third of the meringue mixture.
Pipe small (3–4-cm/1¼–1½-inch)

meringues onto a prepared baking sheet
in spirals. Try to make them all roughly
the same size.

Repeat this process with another third
of the meringue mixture, using a
different colour in the piping bag.

Fill the third piping bag with the
remaining meringue mixture and pipe
plain, uncoloured swirls of meringue
onto the third baking sheet and scatter
sprinkles lightly over the plain meringues.

Bake all the meringues in the preheated
oven for about 40–45 minutes. You may
need to swap the baking sheets around
the shelves halfway through cooking
so that all the meringues cook evenly.
Remove from the oven and leave to cool
on the baking sheets.

Whip the cream until just stiff, then
spoon into one of the cleaned piping
bags. Pipe the cream onto the base of
half of the meringues. Sandwich with
another meringue and arrange on a
serving dish.

meringue snowflakes

These pretty snowflakes are simply made from a basic meringue, but add a festive touch to any holiday celebration. Dress them up with a sprinkling of edible silver glitter or silver balls.

150 g/³⁄₄ cup caster/superfine sugar
75 g/2¹⁄₂ oz. egg whites (about 2 medium egg whites)
edible silver glitter
edible silver balls

a piping bag fitted with a star nozzle/tip
2 heavy baking sheets, lined with baking parchment

makes 12

Preheat the oven to 200°C (400°F) Gas 6.

Tip the sugar into a small roasting pan and place on the middle shelf of the preheated oven for about 5 minutes or until hot to the touch. When the sugar is ready, turn the oven temperature down to 110°C (225°F) Gas ¹⁄₄.

Meanwhile, whisk the egg whites in the bowl of a stand mixer until frothy. With the motor running on low speed, tip the hot sugar onto the egg whites in one go. Turn the speed up to medium–high and whisk for about 8 minutes or until the meringue is very stiff, white and cold.

Spoon the meringue mixture into the prepared piping bag. Pipe little blobs of meringue onto the prepared baking sheets in the shape of snowflakes. Scatter silver glitter or silver balls over the top.

Bake the meringues in the preheated oven for about 40 minutes, until crisp and dry. Turn off the oven, leave the door closed and let the snowflakes cool down completely inside the oven.

marshmallows & other small treats

Discover, here, a wealth of cute confections — from exotic Turkish delight and rose marzipan dates to traditional vanilla blueberry fudge and retro coconut ice candy. Chocaholics will delight in heather honey truffles and chocolate dipped fruits while kids will go crazy for popcorn lollipops. And why not experiment with the marshmallows? They are so versatile, and can be enjoyed in hot cocoa, s'mores or just on their own. Once you have mastered the basic recipe overleaf, you will see just how easy it is to prepare endless delicious variations — recipes include peppermint, cafe mocha and strawberry malt, but there is nothing to stop you swirling, coating, dusting or floating your marshmallows any way you please!

basic vanilla marshmallows

Many cooks are intimidated by the idea of marshmallows, but in reality they are incredibly simple to make. This recipe is easy to follow and is the base for the flavour variations on the following pages. Once you have mastered it, you can experiment with your own flavours too, choosing to swirl, coat, dust or float your marshmallow to your heart's desire.

180 g/1½ cups icing/
    confectioners' sugar, plus an
    extra 30 g/¼ cup for dusting
60 g/½ cup cornflour/cornstarch
light vegetable oil, for greasing
240 ml/1 cup ice-cold water
3 tablespoons powdered gelatine
400 g/2 cups granulated sugar
120 ml/½ cup golden syrup/
    light corn syrup
¼ teaspoon fine salt
1 teaspoon vanilla extract

*a rectangular metal baking pan
    (33 x 22 x 5 cm/13 x 9 x 2 inches)
a sugar thermometer*

makes 45

In a large mixing bowl, sift the 180 g/1½ cups of the icing/confectioners' sugar together with the cornflour/cornstarch and set aside.

Oil the bottom and sides of the baking pan, wiping it down with paper towels to remove any excess oil. Dust the bottom and sides of the pan liberally with the sifted icing/confectioners' sugar and cornflour/cornstarch mixture.

Pour half of the water into a large mixing bowl and sprinkle the gelatine over the water. Leave to stand for about 10 minutes.

Warm the granulated sugar, golden syrup/light corn syrup, remaining water and salt in a large saucepan set over low heat, stirring continuously with a wooden spoon until the sugar has dissolved. Increase the heat to medium–high and boil for 10–12 minutes, or until a sugar thermometer reaches 116°C/240°F (this is known as the soft ball stage). Remove the pan from the heat and pour in the gelatine mixture. Stir with a wooden spoon until the gelatine has dissolved.

Use an electric hand whisk to beat the mixture on a high setting for 10 minutes, until thick, shiny and tripled in size. Add the vanilla extract and mix again until just combined, then pour into the greased and sugared baking pan, working as quickly as possible.

Sift the remaining 30 g/¼ cup icing/confectioners' sugar evenly over the top and let the marshmallow set at room temperature for at least 4 hours, and up to 1 day until firm.

When the marshmallow is set, turn out onto a chopping board and cut into cubes.

peppermint marshmallows

1 quantity Basic Vanilla
   Marshmallows (see page 134)
2 teaspoons peppermint extract
red food colouring
crushed candy canes, to decorate

a rectangular metal baking pan
   (33 x 22 x 5 cm/13 x 9 x 2 inches)
a sugar thermometer

makes 45

Peppermint marshmallows are a refreshing yet sweet treat and delicious with a cup of hot chocolate. Top them with a sprinkle of crushed candy canes and present them in a box tied with a ribbon for a cute festive gift.

Prepare the marshmallows according to the recipe for Basic Vanilla Marshmallows on page 134, adding the peppermint extract along with the vanilla extract.

Using a spatula, mix 4 or 5 drops of the food colouring into the marshmallow mixture to create a swirl, taking care not to stir it in completely. Carefully pour the swirled mixture into the prepared baking pan and spread evenly.

Sift the remaining 30 g/¼ cup icing/confectioners' sugar evenly over the top and let the marshmallow set at room temperature for at least 4 hours, and up to 1 day until firm.

When the marshmallow is set, turn out onto a chopping board and cut into cubes. Top with with crushed candy canes, to decorate.

cafe mocha marshmallows

1 quantity Basic Vanilla
   Marshmallows (see page 134)
1 tablespoon instant ground
   coffee
cocoa powder, to serve

*a rectangular metal baking pan
   (33 x 22 x 5 cm/13 x 9 x 2 inches)*
a sugar thermometer

makes 45

These delicious treats have the rich, deep flavour of a cup of coffee with cream and sugar. Serve them floating on top of a hot cup of black coffee dusted with cocoa powder for a chocolate mocha treat. They also make a great addition to a cappuccino or latte instead of whipped cream.

Prepare the marshmallows according to the recipe for Basic Vanilla Marshmallows on page 134, adding the instant ground coffee to the water and gelatine mixture, before leaving to stand for 10 minutes.

When the marshmallow is set, turn out onto a chopping board and cut into cubes. Serve floating on top of hot cups of black coffee, dusted with cocoa powder. Alternatively, dust with ground cinnamon to add a touch of spice.

strawberry malted marshmallows

300 g/2 cups fresh strawberries
2 tablespoons malt powder
1 quantity Basic Vanilla
   Marshmallows (see page 134
   but follow method here)
finely ground, freeze-dried
   strawberries mixed with a
   little cornflour/cornstarch
   (optional)

*a rectangular metal baking pan
   (33 x 22 x 5 cm/13 x 9 x 2 inches)*
a sugar thermometer

makes 45

Strawberry malts are an old-time soda fountain favourite. This recipe takes a strawberry marshmallow and mixes it with malt powder to create a tasty and colourful nod to summer. You will need malt powder, not sweetened malted milk.

To make the strawberry purée, hull the strawberries and cut them into 2.5-cm/1-inch pieces. Put them in a small saucepan set on the stovetop over low heat and cook for 5 minutes. Remove from the heat and leave to cool. When cool, transfer to a food processor and process until puréed. Strain the purée through a sieve/strainer.

Mix the strawberry purée with the malt powder and set the mixture aside.

Prepare the marshmallows according to the recipe for Basic Vanilla Marshmallows on page 134, reducing the quantity of cold water to 180 ml/³⁄₄ cup and adding the strawberry purée and malt mixture to the water and gelatine, before leaving to stand for 10 minutes.

When the marshmallow is set, turn out onto a chopping board and cut into cubes. Coat with the freeze-dried strawberry mixture, if desired.

vanilla blueberry fudge

500 g/2½ cups caster/granulated sugar
200 ml/¾ cup plus 1 tablespoon double/heavy cream
60 g/½ stick butter
1 teaspoon vanilla extract
85 g/¾ cup dried blueberries

a sugar thermometer (optional)
a baking pan (20 cm/8 inches square), greased

makes 64

Fudge is a wonderfully simple pleasure that everyone loves. There's something appealing and nostalgic about it — so why not look out for small jars in which to pile your fudge, like old-fashioned candy jars, then top them with pretty fabric or paper doilies and a sprig of leaves or flowers.

Put the sugar, cream and butter in a large saucepan and heat very gently, stirring occasionally until the butter has melted and the sugar dissolved. Bring the mixture to the boil, without stirring, and continue to heat gently until the mixture reaches 118°C (240°F). (If you don't have a sugar thermometer, drop a little of the syrup into a glass of chilled water. It should keep it's shape and form a soft, flexible ball.)

When the syrup is ready, take the saucepan off the heat and stir in the vanilla extract. Beat the mixture until it thickens, then stir in the blueberries. Tip the mixture into the prepared cake pan and spread it evenly, smoothing down with a palette knife. Leave to cool completely.

When cooled and set, turn the fudge out onto a chopping board and cut into cubes.

turkish delight

2 tablespoons rosewater

pink food colouring

4 tablespoons powdered gelatine

700 g/3½ cups caster/granulated
   sugar

2 tablespoons icing/
   confectioners' sugar

1 tablespoon cornflour/
   cornstarch

*a baking pan (20 cm/8 inches
   square), greased*

makes 64

Glistening cubes of pale pink Turkish delight, delicately scented with rosewater, make a wonderful sweet treat to enjoy after a meal. Or, a few cubes placed in a decorative box tied up with ribbon, perhaps with a few dried rose petals, makes a delightfully romantic gift.

Put 400 ml/1⅔ cups water in a large saucepan set over a low heat and add the rosewater and a few drops of food colouring to make a vibrant pink. Sprinkle over the gelatine and sugar and heat gently, stirring occasionally, until the sugar has dissolved. Bring the liquid to the boil, then reduce the heat and simmer gently for 20 minutes.

When the mixture is ready, remove the pan from the heat and leave to cool for a couple of minutes. Skim off any foam from the top of the mixture then pour it into the prepared baking pan. Cover with clingfilm/plastic wrap and leave to set for 3 hours in the refrigerator.

When set, turn the Turkish delight out onto a chopping board and cut into cubes. Combine the icing/confectioners' sugar and cornflour/cornstarch then sift onto a large plate and toss each cube of Turkish delight in the sugar mixture to coat.

hazelnut & almond praline clusters

115 g/½ cup plus 1 tablespoon
   granulated sugar
60 g/½ cup hazelnuts
60 g/⅔ cup flaked or split
   blanched almonds

a large baking sheet, greased
8 cellophane bags and decorative
   ties (optional)

makes 8 packages

These golden, nutty caramel bites taste divine and look gorgeous gift-wrapped in simple cellophane packages tied simply with ribbon or decorated with other ornaments, such as these cute buttons. Break into small pieces and apportion several per package, or break off larger chunks and serve as it is.

Put the sugar in a large, heavy-based saucepan and heat gently over a low–medium heat, without stirring, until the sugar starts to melt. At this point, stir to mix thoroughly and continue to heat until clear and pale golden.

Add the hazelnuts and almonds to the pan, stir and cook for about 1 minute.

Tip the caramel-coated nuts out onto the prepared baking sheet, spreading out gently. Leave to cool for about 20 minutes before breaking into pieces.

If packaging, make sure the nuts are completely cool first. Otherwise, store the praline clusters in an airtight container until ready to serve.

rose marzipan dates

25 plump fresh dates
200 g/1⅓ cups ground almonds
100 g/⅔ cup icing/confectioners'
    sugar, sifted
freshly squeezed lemon juice
2 tablespoons rosewater

to decorate
caster/superfine sugar
freshly toasted flaked almonds,
    chopped
fresh rose petals, crystallized
    roses or dried rosebuds

makes 25

Luxuriate in the delicate, subtle character of these romantic flavours. As well as toasted almonds, try decorating the dates with fresh edible roses, crystallized roses or dried rosebuds, or rolling them in sugar.

Slit the dates open lengthways and remove the stones/pits.

Put the icing/confectioners' sugar and ground almonds in a large mixing bowl. Make a well in the centre and add a little lemon juice and the rosewater. Gradually combine the dry and wet ingredients, using a cold fork to work the mixture into a firm paste. It may appear initially that there is not enough moisture, but eventually the almonds will release their natural oils.

Divide the marzipan equally between the dates and decorate as desired.

coconut ice candy

a 397-g/14-oz. can sweetened
   condensed milk
350 g/3½ cups unsweetened
   desiccated/dried shredded
   coconut
375 g/3 cups icing/confectioners'
   sugar, sifted
pink food colouring

a baking pan (20 cm/8 inches
   square), greased

makes 64

*There's something wonderfully nostalgic about coconut ice
and it can bring a deliciously kitsch and slightly cheeky feel to
a celebration spread. Traditionally, coconut ice is pink and
white striped and will look gorgeous piled up on little glass
cake stands decorated with ribbon.*

Put the condensed milk, coconut and
icing/confectioners' sugar in a large
mixing bowl and stir well to combine.
It will make a very stiff mixture so will
require a bit of work. Spoon half of the
mixture into the prepared baking pan
and spread out in an even layer, pressing
down well with the back of a spoon.

Add a few drops of pink food colouring
to the remaining mixture and stir well to

combine, adding more food colouring if
necessary to achieve the desired shade.

Spoon the pink mixture on top of the
white and spread out evenly, pressing
down well with the back of a spoon.
Cover with clingfilm/plastic wrap and
leave to set overnight.

Once set, turn the coconut ice out onto
a chopping board and cut into cubes.

heather honey truffles

100 g/3½ oz. dark/bittersweet
  chocolate (70% cocoa solids),
  chopped
50 g/1¼ oz. milk chocolate
  (35–40% cocoa solids),
  chopped
75 ml/5 tablespoons whipping
  cream
1 tablespoon heather honey

to decorate
200 g/7 oz. dark/bittersweet
  chocolate (70% cocoa solids)
golden caster/superfine or
  sanding sugar

a piping bag fitted with a 12-mm/
  ½-inch nozzle/tip
2 baking sheets, lined with baking
  parchment

makes 20–25

Rich, dark chocolate is delicious in combination with floral heather honey. Use a local heather honey to make this truffle personal to your part of the world.

Chop both the dark and milk chocolate into small pieces and put in a large heatproof bowl. Set the bowl over a pan of barely simmering water to let the chocolate just soften. Take off the heat when soft but not totally liquid.

Put the cream and honey in a saucepan. Heat gently until it just comes to the boil and stir gently. Take the pan off the heat and wait for the mixture to stop bubbling before pouring it over the softened chocolate in the bowl. Stir the chocolate and cream together until they blend into a thick chocolate ganache. Chill the ganache in the fridge for at least 1 hour, until firm.

Whisk the chilled ganache with an electric hand whisk for a few minutes until light and mousse-like. If it is too chilled and has set solid, you will need to whisk for a little longer. Be careful not to overwhisk though as it could start to split.

Spoon the whipped ganache into the prepared piping bag and pipe little balls onto one of the prepared baking sheets. Transfer the baking sheet to the refrigerator and chill the truffles for 15 minutes, until they are firm.

The truffles are now ready to decorate. Spread the sugar out on a tray.

Melt the chocolate in a heatproof bowl set over a pan of simmering water. Using a fork, dip each truffle ball into the melted chocolate. Gently tap the fork on the edge of the bowl to help remove excess chocolate from the truffle.

Carefully put the dipped truffle on the finishing tray and check that it is totally sealed with chocolate – use the fork to cover any holes. Sprinkle the sugar over the top of the truffles with a spoon, then gently roll them in the sugar. Don't be tempted to roll them too soon as the chocolate will take a few minutes to set firm enough. Transfer the finished truffles to the other baking sheet as you work.

Repeat until all the truffles are coated, then leave them to set completely before serving.

delicious dipped fruits

about 30 bite-size pieces of fresh fruit, such as cherries, strawberries, kiwi, apricots, peaches and physalis (cape gooseberries)

200 g/7 oz. dark/bittersweet chocolate (70% cocoa solids), chopped

1–2 baking sheets, lined with baking parchment

serves 4–6

Dipping juicy fruits in dark chocolate is not only easy to do, but a relatively healthy sweet treat and also dairy-free. This couldn't be simpler. Choose the fruits you wish to eat, melt some chocolate, dip and go!

Wash and prepare the fruit as necessary. If using strawberries, cherries and/or physalis, do leave the stalks and hulls on. Pat well with paper towels to remove any excess water.

Melt the chocolate in a heatproof bowl set over a pan of simmering water. Carefully dip each piece of fruit halfway into the chocolate, tap it on the side of the bowl to remove any excess chocolate, and put on the prepared baking sheets. Transfer the baking sheets to a cool place and leave to set.

These fruits should be eaten on the day they are made and stored in the fridge until you are ready to serve.

Variation: For Dipped Dried Fruits choose a good selection of 24–30 naturally sun-dried fruits, such as: apricots, dates, pineapple, pear, chewy banana chips, mangoes, figs and prunes.

popcorn lollipops

Kids love lollipops and these delicious popcorn–mallow ones are sure to make them smile. They take no time at all to prepare and look very cheerful decorated with pretty coloured sprinkles, if you wish.

1–2 tablespoons sunflower or vegetable oil
50 g/3 tablespoons popcorn kernels
200 g/4 cups marshmallows
40 g/3 tablespoons butter
icing/confectioners' sugar, for dusting
sugar sprinkles (optional)

a silicone mat (optional)
10 lollipop/popsicle sticks

makes 10

Heat the oil in a large lidded saucepan with a few popcorn kernels in the pan. When you hear the kernels pop, carefully tip in the rest of the kernels. Shake the pan over the heat until the popping stops. Take care when lifting the lid as any unpopped kernels may still pop from the heat of the pan. Tip the popcorn into a bowl, removing any unpopped kernels as you go.

Heat the marshmallows and butter in a saucepan set over gentle heat, stirring all the time, until both have melted. Take care that the mixture does not burn.

Pour over the popcorn and stir through so that every kernel is evenly coated. Leave to cool for 20 minutes.

Dusting your hands well with icing/confectioners' sugar (this will help prevent the marshmallow sticking to them), shape the mixture into 10 balls about the size of a clementine or small orange. Place the balls on a silicone mat or sheet of baking parchment and insert a lollipop/popsicle stick into each. Sprinkle each lollipop with sugar sprinkles, if using, and leave to set for several hours before serving.

index

recipe credits

Susannah Blake
Cherry Biscotti
Coconut Ice Candy
Floral Baby Cake Bites
Hazelnut and Almond Praline Clusters
Meringue Kisses
Mini Cupcakes
Ribboned Sugar Cookies
Turkish Delight
Vanilla Blueberry Fudge
White Chocolate Cake Pops

Claire Burnet
Delicious Dipped Fruits
Heather Honey Truffles
Very Berry Chocolate Brownies

Maxine Clark
Chocolate and Pistachio Meringues

Julian Day
Butterfly Cakes
Lemon Cookies

Lydia France
Rose Marzipan Dates

Carol Hilker
Basic Vanilla Marshmallows
Cafe Mocha Marsmallows
Peppermint Marshmallows
Strawberry Malted Marshmallows

Hannah Miles
Almond and Amaretto Pies
Baby Eclairs
Blackcurrant Millefeuilles
Caramel Paris Brest
Caramelized Tartes au Citron
Chocolate Profiteroles
Chocolate and Salted Caramel Tartlets
Coconut Doughnuts
French Fancies
Glazed Sprinkle Doughnuts
Individual Plum Tartes Tatin
Ice Cream Whoopie Pies
Lemon Ring Doughnuts
Little Maids of Honour
Mini Blueberry Bundts
Mini Carrot Muffins
Mini Lemon and Lime Meringue Pies
Peanut Butter and Jelly Pies
Pistachio Doughnuts
Popcorn Cookies
Popcorn Lollipops
Raspberry Ring Doughnuts
Rose Petal Religieuses

Rose and Violet Cream Pies
Strawberry and Cream Layer Cakes
Summer Berry Tartlets
Traditional Jam Doughnuts
Vanilla Whoopie Pies
Yum Yums

Annie Rigg
Apple and Blackberry Macarons
Apricot and Almond Macarons
Blueberry and Vanilla Macarons
Brookies
Brownie Pops
Cappucino Macarons
Cherry and Coconut Brownies
Chocolate and Passion Fruit Macarons
Coffee Blondies
Gingerbread Dancing Shoes
Iced Gem Cakes
Lilac and Lavender Petits Fours
Mint Chocolate Kisses
Meringue Snowflakes
Petits Fours Brownies
Rose Macarons
Salted Caramel Macarons
Summer Berry Cupcakes
Super-duper Disco Meringues

picture credits

All illustrations by: **Maria Lee-Warren**

Food Photography by:

Carolyn Barber
Pages 1, 4–5, 8 above left and right, 13,
22–23, 30 insert, 32 below left, 34–35,
38–39, 45 background, 108 above left,
124–125, 143, 144, 146–147, 151

Martin Brigdale
Pages 46–47 background, 57, 83, 93, 142

Peter Cassidy
Pages 108 below left, 126

Jean Cazals
Page 148

Laura Edwards
Pages 32 above left and right, 47 insert,
48 insert, 52–53, 55 insert, 56 insert

Tara Fisher
Pages 43–44, 45 insert, 156

Jonathan Gregson
Pages 51, 132 below right, 152, 155

Lisa Linder
Page 130

William Lingwood
Pages 6, 8 below left and right, 18–19,
30–31 background, 49, 54–55 background, 58 above left and right, 60–71,

73, 80–81 background, 84, 86–92,
94–101, 103–105, 107, 110–111 background, 113, 120, 134, 138, 145, 149,
154, 157

Steve Painter
Pages 20–21, 40–42, 58 below left and
right, 74–75, 77–79, 81 insert, 82, 132
above left and right and below left,
135–137, 139–141

Kate Whitaker
Pages 2–3, 7, 9–11, 14–17, 24–29, 32
below right, 33, 36, 59, 85, 108 above
right and below right, 109, 111 insert,
112, 114–119, 121–122, 128–129, 131,
133, 153

Clare Winfield
Pages 123, 150

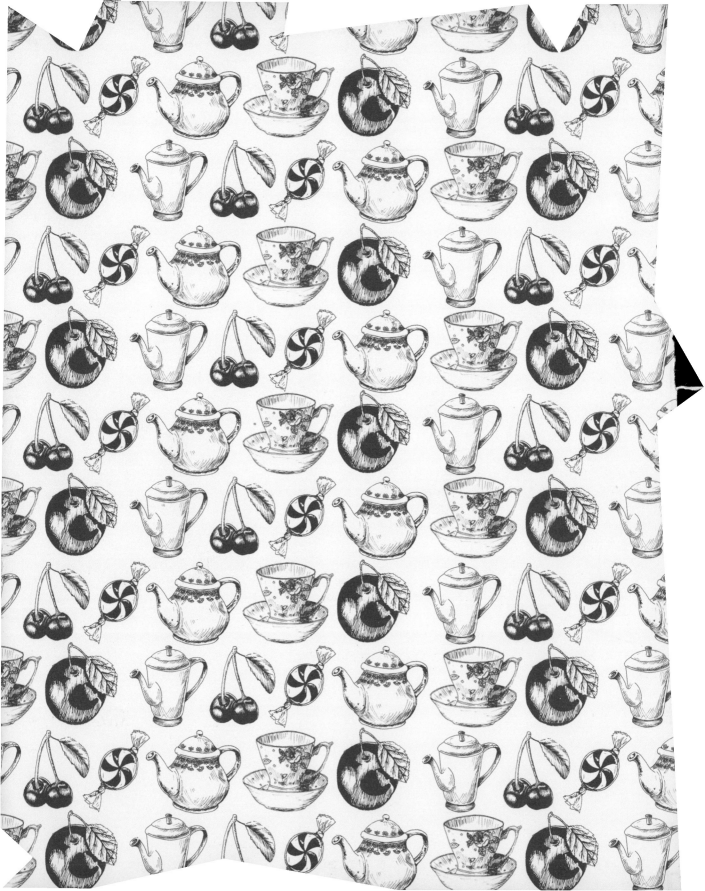